Critical Literacy

Context, Research, and Practice
in the K–12 Classroom

Lisa Patel Stevens
Boston College

Thomas W. Bean
University of Nevada, Reno

SAGE Publications
Thousand Oaks ▪ London ▪ New Delhi

Copyright © 2007 by Sage Publications, Inc.

All rights reserved. No part of this book may be reproduced or utilized in any form or by any means, electronic or mechanical, including photocopying, recording, or by any information storage and retrieval system, without permission in writing from the publisher.

For information:

Sage Publications, Inc.
2455 Teller Road
Thousand Oaks, California 91320
E-mail: order@sagepub.com

Sage Publications Ltd.
1 Oliver's Yard
55 City Road
London, EC1Y 1SP
United Kingdom

Sage Publications India Pvt. Ltd.
B-42, Panchsheel Enclave
Post Box 4109
New Delhi 110 017 India

Printed in the United States of America.

Library of Congress Cataloging-in-Publication Data

Patel Stevens, Lisa.
Critical literacy : context, research, and practice in the K-12 classroom / Lisa P. Stevens, Thomas W. Bean.
 p. cm.
Includes bibliographical references and index.
ISBN-13: 978-1-4129-4117-4 (cloth)
ISBN-13: 978-1-4129-4118-1 (pbk.)
 1. Critical pedagogy—United States. 2. Literacy—Social aspects—United States. I. Bean, Thomas W. II. Title.

LC196.5.U6P37 2007
302.2'244—dc22   2006028037

This book is printed on acid-free paper.

07   08   09   10   11   10   9   8   7   6   5   4   3   2   1

Acquiring Editor:	Diane McDaniel
Editorial Assistant:	Erica Carroll
Project Editor:	Astrid Virding
Copy Editor:	Barbara Coster
Typesetter:	C&M Digitals (P) Ltd.
Proofreader:	Kevin Gleason
Indexer:	Juniee Oneida
Cover Designer:	Michelle Kenny

Critical
Literacy

In gratitude to my mother, my first and best teacher,
the one who taught me so much by example: how to love,
how to pursue my happiness, and how to trust my sense of myself.

—Lisa

I wish to acknowledge my partner and colleague, Dr. Helen J. Harper,
who makes every day a new adventure with boundless possibilities. In addition,
I want to extend appreciation to my past, present, and future doctoral students
at the University of Nevada, Las Vegas who, by continually striving to discover
new directions in literacy research, move my thinking forward as well.

—Tom

Contents

Foreword

Critical literacy is concerned with critiquing relationships among language use, social practice, and power. It is an analytic process that is mediated by one's worldview or theory and that closely examines the ways in which language practices carve up the world according to certain socially valued criteria (and not other sets of criteria). It draws attention to inequities and calls for a rethinking of ideas and social assumptions considered "natural" or unassailable. Historically speaking, critical literacy has its roots reaching deep into critical theory, philosophy, linguistics, and discourse studies. Within English-speaking countries, the translation and publication of Paulo Friere's work to English in the 1970s, along with his collaborations with Donaldo Macedo and Ira Shor, mark a watershed in the development of critical literacy as a distinct theoretical and pedagogical field. This work focused educators' attention on the importance of identifying authentic social problems and ways of addressing these problems through language and action. In the second half of the 1980s, Gunther Kress and Robert Hodges's work in critical discourse analysis was also to prove highly influential in the development of critical literacy.

The term *critical literacy* itself, however, is a relatively recent development. Used in the 1980s by people like Ira Shor and Joe Kretovics, its first appearance as a book title came only in 1993 with the publication of Colin Lankshear and Peter McLaren's edited collection, *Critical Literacy: Politics, Praxis and the Postmodern* (published by the State University of New York Press). This collection drew attention to the multiplicity of ways of being literate and the complex ways in which literacy is tied to and shaped by power. Lankshear and McLaren's volume drew together a diverse group of scholars across a range of fields and disciplines (e.g., feminist theory, sociolinguistics, philosophy, ethnography) and underscored the extent to which critical literacy is not a unitary, neatly bounded approach to literacy practice and pedagogy.

During the mid- to late 1990s, critical literacy gained momentum and took on the characteristics of an education movement, especially in Australia, New Zealand, South Africa, and England. Within these countries, critical literacy proved influential at a range of institutional levels, spanning theoretical development work, teacher education, state and national policies, national funding initiatives, regional professional development initiatives, and classroom practice. Despite the various (per)mutations critical literacy underwent as it was absorbed into education and, in many cases, institutionalized in the form of syllabus directives and professional development "kits" and programs, one thing remained in common: the assumption that teaching students how to recognize the ways in which language "operates" in relation to social practices, social groups, and power can make a positive difference in their lives. This assumption goes hand in hand with the recognition that language practices can also constrain and limit students' life chances. Pam Gilbert, a key scholar in the development of critical literacy practices within teacher education and classrooms, argues that the two-sided nature of literacy—its potential to help transform inequities and its ability to reinscribe inequities—is a key component of critical literacy. All too often, however, this duality is not given sufficient attention in the critical literacy literature, where the limiting effects that literacy can have in the school lives of some students seems often to be taken as a given rather than as a place from which to begin analysis and critique.

Lisa Patel Stevens and Tom Bean provide us with a book that insists on contextualizing their discussion of critical literacy within carefully described settings and transcribed exchanges in order to show how potentially limiting ways of reading, writing, and being can be made over into rich learning experiences and spaces for action by means of critical literacy understandings. For example, their opening chapter includes a detailed account of how dominant school (and social) discourses ensure that a Grade 5 science textbook becomes an abstract collection of "facts" to be "learned" by students. These facts have been excised neatly and effectively from the usually messy ethical, sustainable development, ownership, producer-consumer relationships and debates associated with natural resource use and management in real life. The authors explain how one teacher refused to be limited by the schooled nature of the science textbook she was assigned to use in her class. Instead, she structured her teaching so as to use current news events concerning resource shortages to launch her students' critique of the (lack of *real*) information contained in their textbook and to investigate and write up missing information about phenomena like electricity as a market commodity rather than a natural force.

Stevens and Bean use an extensive array of examples throughout their book to "show" what critical literacy is, rather than aiming to provide a single, fixed definition. This substantive approach means they are able to capture the ways in which language practices both shape and are shaped by the worldviews of different social groups and how, all too often, the discourse practices of dominant social groups dictate what can and cannot be "said" or even "seen." The authors argue that critical literacy knowledge and strategies become increasingly important as new forms of literacy practice emerge in association with technological and communication developments occurring in "New Times." Critical literacy has in many ways become textbound. Teachers tend to focus on analyzing and critiquing conventionally printed texts and, to a much lesser degree, film or video texts. As the authors rightly argue, within so-called developed countries this text-centric view of critical literacy is fast reaching its use-by date. Stevens and Bean call for a broadening of critical literacy practices within education to take account of "new literacy" developments such as the increasing significance of attention economies, multimodal resources for information and communication purposes, and the increasing mobility and shrinkage of communication and information devices. They argue that critical literacy practitioners can no longer afford to think only locally but need to pay attention to the social, cultural, and economic effects of globalization on language use, opportunity, and power.

Part of this context is the increased accountability being placed on teachers within the United States (and elsewhere) to ensure their students (a) are able to "read" by the end of Grade 3, (b) meet state-level standards, and (c) "pass" a range of standardized tests. Stevens and Bean remind us of how policy-mandated reading practices and pronouncements present a particular version of what it means to "be a reader" and what it means to read well at school, and how these versions can actually work to limit students' options for academic success. The authors describe how a contextualized conception of reading acts as a valuable counterfoil to policy and curriculum packages that insist on defining "literacy" as the ability to merely encode and decode print. Equally important, Stevens and Bean also rail against the ongoing deprofessionalization of teachers by means of one-size-fits-all "scripted" literacy curricula and by the reduction of "successful" teaching to high student "pass" rates on standardized tests. Their book models for teachers and teacher educators ways both of *teaching* critical literacy insights and strategies to students and of *practicing* critical literacy themselves, such that they can find productive gaps and spaces within dumbed-down literacy teaching packages where they can adopt contextualized approaches to literacy education and act as agents of beneficial change. The authors provide concrete examples that go to the heart of teachers' everyday working lives. These include accounts of teachers actively researching, analyzing, and critiquing a proposed new literacy curriculum package for their school and of teachers using critical literacy strategies to challenge new federal literacy policies and the larger discourses that shape these policies and that, in turn, are sustained by them. This insistence that teachers (and teacher educators) can and should both teach critical literacy *and* practice it serves as wise counsel and as a touchstone of hope within New Times—where the "new" doesn't necessarily mean "improved" or "better" times for everyone.

—Michele Knobel
Montclair State University

Preface

> We are all susceptible to the subtle and sometimes not so subtle influences of carefully crafted texts aimed at enticing us to buy a product or to buy into a particular political ideology or social practice. For example, a laptop computer review touts the Itronix Hummer Laptop as "the in-your-face status symbol for the ultimate road warrior" (Malloy, 2006, p. 146). Indeed, the photo accompanying the review shows a tough-looking yellow and black laptop computer that looks suspiciously like its automotive namesake. The ad goes on to say that this laptop will turn heads but cautions, "Just don't bring it to a Greenpeace rally" (p. 146). Overall, it earns a high rating for durability and performance. What audience do you think this ad is aimed at? Would you purchase this computer? Why? Why not? And, as a reader, how are you being viewed by the writer of this ad?

This brief scenario offers a glimpse at the process of critiquing various forms of text, in this case, a computer review published in a magazine for laptop users, particularly users traveling a great deal on business. At a more advanced level, students need to be able to apply critical literacy to a host of texts spanning not just advertisements but also textbooks, media, newscasts, political treatises, historical accounts, scientific accounts, and the increasing array of international and global items that are featured in the news.

You may be wondering why we decided to write a book on critical literacy amid a political climate where high-stakes testing may result in decisions that create curriculum far too narrow in scope for the development of informed citizens. We both bring experiences to this project based on our work with teachers in classrooms where we have seen the results of equipping students with the tools to critique a wide range of discourse, including films, novels, texts, advertisements, songs, and other forms of text. We also spend considerable time staying abreast of futuristic thinking about education in a global geopolitical context that will, in our estimation, require citizens able to discern how they are being positioned, and at times manipulated by the media and the Internet, as well as more traditional texts. This combination of classroom experience and theoretical grounding provides the foundation for our work in critical literacy and the ideas and practices we recommend throughout the book. Moreover, any nostalgic view of literacy based on traditional texts is, in our view, myopic. Students are bombarded by a huge range of text forms and new literacies. These new literacies include "performative, visual, aural, and semiotic elements in print and non-print texts" (Alvermann, 2002, p. viii). Semiotics refers to sign systems, including fonts, diagrams, symbols, and other elements of discourse, that may be perceived and interpreted in various ways by a reader or viewer (Van Leeuwen, 2005). New literacies classrooms are generally characterized by students engaged in daily work in multiple forms of representation, including multimedia PowerPoints, WebQuests, i-movies, and so on (Kist, 2005). In addition, the teacher and students conduct explicit discussions of why certain symbol systems socially construct meaning in particular ways. Collaboration, critique, and a high degree of engagement where time passes fluidly typify these classrooms (Kist, 2005). In this new literacies environment, we believe that equipping students with the tools for engaging in critical literacy is becoming a necessity for leading an informed life in our global world.

A RATIONALE FOR CRITICAL LITERACY

The next time you go to a car dealership with a showroom where you might be waiting to get your car serviced, have a look at the brochures advertising various models. These ads invite the reader to envision what it might be like to own a particular model of car. In essence, they position the reader in particular ways in terms of gender, age, and class. In fact, these sorts of advertisements offer a form of discourse that helps us grasp some of the elements of critical literacy. Consider the following excerpt from a brochure featuring the latest version of the popular Mazda Miata sports car (Mazda North American Operations, 2004):

> The Mazda MX-5 Miata's cockpit is designed to facilitate a single function. The unobstructed communication between man and machine. To that end, its leather-wrapped steering wheel awaits your input. (p. 9)

In the process of deconstructing and critiquing this ad, it is immediately apparent that the reader has been socially constructed as a male persona interested in a very visceral connection to the highway, and this sports car offers that experience. The car is clearly not for hauling the soccer team to its Saturday game or car-topping a windsurfer to the lake. Nevertheless, many women drive Mazda Miatas, and their popularity is certainly not limited to male drivers interested in wrenching the car into a four-wheel drift through a city street. Thus, we can, using the tools of critical literacy, deconstruct and critique many forms of discourse, including ads, films, novels, music lyrics, and more traditional texts. But it is important to note that there are times when a film or novel, or a sports car, for that matter, should just be experienced and enjoyed. With that caveat in mind, we do believe that critical literacy offers a powerful means for students to become more aware of how multiple texts are constructed and how they influence our thinking. But why, as we said earlier, does this matter if all students need to do to succeed in life is pass low-level tests that simply do not require critical literacy?

Globalization and Informed Decision Making

The world landscape is, in the view of Pulitzer Prize–winning *New York Times* columnist Thomas Friedman (2005), becoming flat through the interconnectedness of global communications. "We are entering a phase where we are going to see the digitization, virtualization, and automation of almost everything" (p. 45). For example, *Wikipedia*, the peoples' encyclopedia, now outpaces former print-based encyclopedias in use with a totally open system of comment and critique. But that feature assumes, or at least necessitates, a citizenry well educated and critical enough to offer insightful and accurate critique. The dark side of the Internet requires global citizens who are able to see how they are being positioned by multiple texts offered in this fluid and pervasive medium. Friedman notes:

> The Internet is an enormously useful tool for the dissemination of propaganda, conspiracy theories, and plain old untruths, because it combines a huge reach with a patina of technology that makes anything on the Internet somehow more believable. (p. 432)

We do not want to imply that it is just the Internet that presents discourse worth examining through a critical literacy lens. All forms of discourse can be scrutinized through critical literacy if students have the metalanguage and analytical tools needed to accomplish such an analysis. For example, Nel

Noddings (2005) visited classrooms where young students were researching where their toys were constructed and the degree to which child labor was involved. Noddings argued that "[e]very citizen should acquire an understanding of propaganda and its power to influence opinion" (p. 130).

METALANGAUGE AND THE TOOLS OF CRITICAL LITERACY

In any discipline or activity, including sports, music, and so on, insiders know the metalanguage commonly used to discuss elements of the relevant activity. For example, surfers have a well-honed array of words to characterize wave conditions: *glassy, choppy, gnarly, closed out.* The technical vocabulary associated with critical literacy has its own "insiders'" jargon or metalanguage. Critical literacy has its own metalanguage that assists students in deconstructing the hidden messages or underlying agendas and power differentials in any discourse. In order to help you and your students become insiders in critical literacy, we will list just a few of the key terms that we use throughout the book. But first, it's important to specify what we mean by *critical literacy.*

Critical literacy: Critical literacy views text meaning-making as a process of social construction with a particularly critical eye toward elements of the various historical, social, and political contexts that permeate and foreground any discourse. In order to further refine this definition, we need to look at what discourse is being critiqued and how one assumes a critical literacy stance.

Discourse: Any text, film, song, poem, or advertisement (and other discourse forms) is never neutral. That is, discourse always has an underlying agenda, and any discourse can be examined and deconstructed to determine who has a voice in the discourse, who is silenced by it or marginalized, and how these gaps and silences can be transformed.

Positioning: Authors, filmmakers, song writers, ad writers, and so on produce discourse that positions the reader in various ways. For example, reality television places the viewer in a voyeuristic position, looking in on the foibles of various actors. Self-help books with the now familiar but derogatory title *Sailing (Computing, Poker Playing,* etc.) *for Dummies* targets the neophyte in any activity. These books have been around for some time, but most of us are reluctant to be seen at the bookstore counter waving our *Cooking* (or whatever) *for Dummies* books around. These books position us as outsiders in an activity.

Texts as cultural tools: When we see ourselves represented in the texts we read, this recognition impacts our identity. Texts can establish belonging or alienation. In essence, texts are sites where some groups are included and others excluded. Thus, we can ask of any text: Who is represented? Who is excluded? Who has power? Who is denied power?

Texts as sites for multiple interpretations: The now widely cited example of varying interpretations of Columbus and the "discovery" of America is a good example of how social class, gender, and ethnicity influence our reading and interpretation of texts. On the one hand, the European American celebration of this discovery is a common interpretation, but it has been challenged in post-colonial discourse from a Native American or First Nations perspective. Thus, critical literacy offers a means to compare and contrast varying interpretations of any discourse.

Critical media literacy: Critical media literacy refers to the application of the deconstructive elements of critical literacy to media texts (e.g., songs, ads, billboards, brochures for products) often encountered outside the classroom. Indeed, popular culture is a pervasive part of students' lives and offers engaging sites for the application of critical literacy practices.

Critical policy analysis: This critical literacy stance recognizes that policies (e.g., No Child Left Behind) are ideological in nature, contextualized in terms of political, historical, and economic dimensions, and subject to analysis, critique, and deconstruction.

While you will encounter other key terms in each chapter, we wanted to foreshadow a few of the concepts and metalanguage underpinning critical literacy. Indeed, these elements differentiate critical literacy from older notions of critical reading aimed at helping students distinguish fact from opinion. We also want to caution that critical literacy is more complex than critical reading and not susceptible to simple procedural descriptions. Critical literacy calls for a habit of mind predisposed to look at discourse and ask: Who has their views represented? Who is privileged in a particular discourse? Who is left out? What social, political, economic, gender, and ethnicity aspects are at play in various forms of discourse? In essence, critical literacy calls for a predisposition to deconstruct and critique all forms of discourse. However, we want to offer one additional caution, and that is, sometimes it's just fine to simply enjoy a poem, song, novel, film, enticing ad, or art of all kinds. Not everything should be deconstructed, and students have their own spaces where they simply need to enjoy the aesthetics of an engaging song, ad, or film.

Throughout the book, we have offered concrete examples of classrooms where critical literacy is an integral part of teachers' repertoires along with more traditional curriculum elements. Toward that end, we have constructed the book in such a way that you can start incorporating critical literacy practices in your classroom at a pace that is right for you and your students. In the section that follows, we highlight the organization of the book and special features we think you will find helpful.

ORGANIZATION OF THE BOOK

We have organized the book into eight chapters. The first three chapters offer foundational information about critical literacy theory along with some classroom examples. Chapter 1, "Redefining Literacy," charts the historical trends in literacy pedagogy and the current heightened need for critical literacy. This chapter also differentiates older forms of critical reading from critical literacy. Chapter 2, "Why We Need Critical Literacy: Dynamic Texts and Identity Formation," situates critical literacy within the broad-based international work on multiliteracies and digital literacies. In Chapter 3, "Critical Literacy and Teacher Education," we consider various aspects of critical literacy within the broader framework of teacher identity and critical media literacy. In addition, we introduce a strategy for critical literacy we call Resident Critic.

Chapters 4 through 7 emphasize issues of practice with classroom examples at various grade levels. Chapter 4, "Critical Literacy at the Nexus of Praxis," introduces key metalinguistic tools of critical literacy and application of these tools through classroom examples. Chapter 5, "Praxis Point 1: Popular Culture, Fandom, and Boundaries," explores the delicate balance involved in including students' out-of-school popular culture interests in the curriculum while respecting their space to engage divergent texts. A classroom scenario helps illustrate some of the issues that need to be addressed when teachers elect to use popular culture materials in the classroom. Chapter 6, "Praxis Point 2: Critical Numeracy Across the Curriculum," offers a classroom example and discussion of how to handle the tensions that exist between project-based learning and critical literacy in a political climate that often mandates lower-level thinking skills. Chapter 7, "Praxis Point 3: Cycles of Deconstruction and Reconstruction," continues the process of illustrating the role of critical literacy in expanding students' grasp of subjectivity and critical literacy in a high school context.

Chapter 8, "Critical Literacy and Educational Policy Texts," provides a primer on critical policy analysis and a close look at the ways in which policy intersects with classroom life for teachers and students. Indeed, the vitality of a curriculum that embraces critical literacy as one cornerstone of students' literacy development is highly dependent upon teachers who can articulate their vision and fend off calls for lowering expectations for students. Chapter 9, "Critical Policy Analysis in Local Contexts," uses the critical policy analysis work from Chapter 8 and examines how policies can be critiqued in specific contexts. The chapter includes a discussion of Foucault's ideas about governmentality to explore how various teachers respond to educational policy, with implications about how to engage in this work in local contexts.

SPECIAL FEATURES OF THE BOOK

We have included various special features that will make your journey into the seemingly complex world of critical literacy much more accessible than you might imagine. For example, each chapter begins with a brief scenario that sets the stage for the concepts to be introduced. These scenarios encapsulate key elements of critical literacy treated in more detail as a chapter unfolds. Throughout the book, *classroom examples* are included, based on our experiences with teachers engaging students in critical literacy in various elementary, middle school, and high school settings. *Specific teaching strategies* for critical literacy are included toward the end of each chapter. These strategies can be integrated into your classroom at a pace that allows for experimentation within your existing curriculum. In each chapter we offer a section titled Key Terms, where definitions of the vocabulary commonly associated with critical literacy are listed in bold-faced print and briefly defined. These terms are used throughout many of the recommended readings listed in this introduction and subsequent chapters. Terms that are in bold can also be found in the Glossary. Finally, Recommended Further Reading sources are included at the close of each chapter. Online resources are listed, along with more traditional books, articles, and monographs.

In summary, we know that pedagogical and curricular change is an incremental process where small steps often yield powerful results in students' literacy growth. We believe strongly that the resources offered in this book will enhance your current teaching and, most important, help students move toward the application of critical literacy. By providing opportunities for critical literacy in and out of the classroom, your students will be acquiring a lifelong predisposition to be unassuming when it comes to the multiple and often conflicting messages they receive from texts, films, novels, the Internet, political figures, and a host of other discourse forms.

RECOMMENDED FURTHER READING

Critical Literacy

Luke, A., & Freebody, P. (1999). Further notes on the four resources model. *Reading Online*. Newark, DE: International Reading Association. Retrieved from www .readingonline.org/research/lukefreebody.html

Critical Media Literacy

Alvermann, D. E., Moon, J. S., & Hagood, M. C. (1999). *Popular culture in the class-room: Teaching and researching critical media literacy.* Newark, DE: International Reading Association.
Van Leeuwen, T. (2005). *Introducing social semiotics.* London: Routledge.

Critical Policy Analysis

Edmondson, J. (2004). *Understanding and applying critical policy analysis: Reading educators advocating for change.* Newark, DE: International Reading Association.
Stevens, L. P. (2003). Reading First: A critical policy analysis. *The Reading Teacher, 56,* 662–672.

Discourse

Gee, J. P. (1996). *Social linguistics and literacies: Ideology and discourse* (2nd ed.). London: Taylor & Francis.

Globalization

Friedman, T. L. (2005). *The world is flat: A brief history of the twenty-first century.* New York: Farrar, Straus & Giroux.
Noddings, N. (2005). What have we learned? In N. Noddings (Ed.), *Educating citizens for global awareness.* New York: Teachers College Press.

New Literacies

Alvermann, D. E. (2002). Preface. In D. E. Alvermann (Ed.), *Adolescents and literacies in a digital world* (pp. vii–xi). New York: Peter Lang.
Kist, W. (2005). *New literacies in action: Teaching and learning in multiple media.* New York: Teachers College Press.
Lankshear, C., & Knobel, M. (2002). Do we have your attention? New literacies, digital technologies, and the education of adolescents. In D. E. Alvermann (Ed.), *Adolescents and literacies in a digital world* (pp. 19–39). New York: Peter Lang.

REFERENCES

Alvermann, D. E. (2002). Preface. In D. E. Alvermann (Ed.), *Adolescents and literacies in a digital world* (pp. vii–xi). New York: Peter Lang.

Friedman, T. L. (2005). *The world is flat: A brief history of the twenty-first century.* New York: Farrar, Straus & Giroux.

Kist, W. (2005). *New literacies in action: Teaching and learning in multiple media.* New York: Teachers College Press.

Malloy, R. (2006, April). Itronix Hummer Laptop: The in-your-face status symbol for the ultimate road warrior. *Laptop: Mobile solutions for business and life, 31*(2), pp. 146–147.

Mazda North American Operations. (2004). *'05 Mazda Miata: Zoom-zoom.* Irvine, CA: Author.

Noddings, N. (2005). What have we learned? In N. Noddings (Ed.), *Educating citizens for global awareness.* New York: Teachers College Press.

Van Leeuwen, T. (2005). *Introducing social semiotics.* London: Routledge.

Acknowledgments

True to our theoretical views of literacy as social practice, the crafting of this book has been a socially constructed work, with many more contributors and interlocutors than just the two of us. We are particularly grateful to the teachers and students who worked with us in exploring how critical literacy can take shape in specific contexts. We continue to be impressed and in awe of the courage it takes not just to teach but to teach for social justice in contemporary times.

In addition, we would like to thank Michele Knobel and Colin Lankshear for the initial support and guidance they provided to early ideas about this book. Michele's consistent feedback was always encouraging while also helping us to push the professional conversation in new directions. Thanks also to Jacqueline Edmondson, who took time to lend her experiential and scholarly voice in a specific contribution. The numerous reviewers of this text have given us invaluable suggestions for revising and editing our early drafts. They include the following:

Patricia E. Calderwood, Fairfield University

Joan C. Fingon, California State University, Los Angeles

Judith A. Gouwens, Roosevelt University

Kathleen A. Hinchman, Syracuse University

Shelley Hong Xu, California State University, Long Beach

Cheryl A. Kreutter, St. John Fisher College

Peter McDermott, The Sage Colleges

Jennifer Moon Ro, Binghamton University-SUNY

Ladislaus M. Semali, Pennsylvania State University

Robert Sylvester, Bridgewater State College

Bogum Yoon, Texas Woman's University

Finally, we would like to thank the staff at Sage Publications who encouraged us throughout the process of creating this text. The guidance of Diane McDaniel was especially critical. In addition, Erica Carroll and Elise Smith were especially helpful in assisting us through the technical aspects of bringing the text to publication. We've been fortunate to have worked with a team of editors who have maintained the central goal of making this a successful and quality product.

CHAPTER 1

Redefining Literacy

A Text-Saturated World

In this chapter we explore varying definitions of literacy, comparing how reading, text, and literacy have come to include different components both in schooling and in society at large. One of the key components that have necessitated revisiting more traditional definitions of literacy is the increase of digital texts in everyday life. Even though print-based texts can be considered multimodal, by varying format and genre, the multitudes of texts produced digitally have pushed new definitions to the forefront of literacy research and practice.

Reflect on your day's activities. Try to recall every instance in which you were interacting with text, written, spoken, or visual. In other words, try to quantify the moments in your day spent conveying or constructing meaning through text.

As you were thinking about the various literacy events that comprise your day, you may or may not have been surprised by the fact that text (spoken, written, visual, printed, electronic) permeates most aspects of our lives. Even when we are engaged in activities that have other than cognitive goals, such as exercising, we often find ourselves dealing with text, such as listening to a portable radio or watching TV. In essence, we are constantly engaged in making meaning from **semiotic**, or signifying, systems, including words, images, and sounds. A semiotic is any type of sign or symbol used to represent an entity. So, anything from letters put together to form a word to corporate logos are semiotics. As consumers and producers of texts, we rely upon these semiotics as a foundation to making meaning. These meaning-making pro-cesses help us to read both the word and the world (Freire, 1970). Because of the exponential growth of mass-mediated and textually driven conduits such as the Internet, we are constantly bombarded by text. And while this simple observation seems to drive home the point that the information age is in full swing, reading and literacy education in the United States often falls short of contending with the far-reaching implications of this expanded definition and confluence of text.

Historically, literacy pedagogy in the United States has followed two strong trends. First, it has focused on the early years of literacy development, implic-itly and explicitly conveying the shortsighted notion that learning to read skills and processes are the most pivotal aspects of literacy pedagogy. Second, liter-acy pedagogy has also tended to vacillate between poles of epistemological grounding, lurching from paradigm to paradigm. Simply put, the field of liter-acy, like many fields in education, swings from one paradigm to another oppo-sitionally posed paradigm. Quintessentially and overly simplistically depicted through the juxtaposition of synthetic phonics-based instruction versus holistic whole language approaches, this vacillation has resulted in the artificial and detrimental segmentation of concurrently complex and codependent literacy skills, processes, and practices. Throughout the Clinton and Bush administra-tions, presidential federal policies guiding funding opportunities to support reading instruction in the United States have been written and implemented to have all students reading by the end of third grade. Undergirding this policy is a narrow definition of reading that focuses strongly on oral reading fluency and automaticity of word calling (Stevens, 2001). This approach to literacy, one that is first limited to decoding and then further focused on oral reading fluency, reflects a dated concept of learning and denies an e-business global-ized economy, one largely mediated through semiotics and textual exchanges (Luke & Luke, 2001). Becoming skilled at decoding the text, while irrefutably essential for any reader to become fluent, is sorely insufficient when not mar-ried with other demands necessary for negotiating today's text-saturated world. The assumption that fast decoding will free attention resources for comprehension denies the necessarily complex and concurrent use of these resources. Such an approach also falls short of negotiating the highly complex and deliberately explicit attention required for dynamic comprehension at fac-tual, affective, and critical levels. For example, being a fluent decoder of text would not, in any way, help a novice user of Internet search engines quickly and strategically move through hundreds of search results, sorting the sources, validity of information, and possible connecting texts. While certainly an essential component to this literacy practice, it is far from being the exclusive or even most important skill.

In fact, strides in literacy research in the past 20 to 30 years should now help educators to better understand not only why some children struggle to succeed with school-sanctioned literacies but also what types of literacy skills, processes, and practices should be included as part of our curricula and pedagogy. One significant finding has been the **intertextual** nature of reading the world through words, including the processes of writing and oral communication. In other words, we construct meaning from the printed word based on our understanding of the world, and these meanings are intertwined among multiples sources of text: books, CDs, conversations, movies, Web sites, video games, pamphlets, TV shows, magazines, and so on (New London Group, 1999).

Another key advance from the 20th century is the debunking of the myth that students spend their elementary years learning to read and then reading to learn in their secondary years. Substantive evidence, found significantly within the field of content area literacy, supports the premise that learning to read is a complex array of skills and processes, modified by the reader to meet the particular content and purpose of a literacy task (e.g., Bean, 2001). This topic is also treated cogently in the International Reading Association's Adolescent Literacy Position Statement (Moore, Bean, Birdyshaw, & Rycik, 1999).

However, arguably the single most salient point that can be drawn from the qualitative research agendas of the latter 20th century and thus far in the 21st century is the highly contextual and relative nature of reading and literacy. Landmark studies such as Shirley Brice Heath's (1983) *Ways With Words* brought home the elegantly simple concept that different communities embrace the negotiation of text in compelling but often wholly different ways. Understanding language and literacy as social practices has helped recent generations of researchers and teachers understand their students as competent meaning makers and has compelled them to find ways to make connections between particular, contextually understood literate practices (e.g., Lewis, 2002; Michaels, 1981; Moje, 2000). Other scholars, such as James Paul Gee, have pointed to the highly contextual nature of discourses, the ways of being, doing, and acting, according to particular situations and participants. At the same time, the electronic age has resulted in a veritable explosion of texts, many of which are conveyed in multiple groups through the media. Mastering the basic skills of decoding falls well short of the demands beckoned through these times. To that end, being a proficient reader can no longer be equated with being able to rapidly decode words in a classroom setting.

Paradoxically, concurrent with this emphasis on code-based definitions of reading, schoolwide programs that rely on repeated readings of decodable text, choral responses, and timed oral reading exercises have grown in popularity. While these trends are alarming for a number of reasons, one of the most basic areas of concern is how reading is defined in these policies.

If reading is defined as an ability to decode text, a skill that can be acquired by the end of third grade, it follows that this performance objective is a rather teleological process based on mastery and rote skill—one in which students gain input from text without engaging in critical **stances.** Such a unitary definition of reading, easily quantified through a precise list of cumulative skills, strategies, and behaviors, has long been critiqued for leading to a deficit view of children and their meaning-making abilities. However, this type of restricted definition also places students, especially those who struggle with school-sanctioned literacies, at a particular disadvantage in a world that is increasingly driven by digital technologies, media saturation, and worldwide marketplaces that rely upon economies of attention (Gee, 1996; New London Group, 1999). Such a definition of reading also erroneously sequences the parallel functions that proficient readers use concurrently to create meaning and critique texts.

It is our contention that we can no longer regard reading as a rudimentary sequence of skills. While the basic skills of decoding, comprehension, and appropriate use of texts have the same essential nature that they have always held, today's hypermediated world demands that we expand our definition of basic skills in reading to include interrelated processes that fit better under the term *literacy*. Also necessary is a revision of our view of what a proficient reader does. While proficient readers certainly are able to orally decode at a fluent rate, they also must be able to comprehend, use text pragmatically, and actively question texts that they encounter.

In particular, the goals of **critical literacy**, being able to tease out various agendas, purposes, and interests represented in texts, are necessary for all of our students, not simply defined as higher-order thinking skills and reserved for those students whom we deem proficient at decoding, and only then if time allows. Instead, aspects of critical literacy must become part and parcel of the definition of comprehension. In essence, by including critical literacy as part of several processes included in literacy, teachers, students, and teacher educators can begin to redraft their literacy instruction to more closely match the highly sophisticated demands of today's world.

GENEALOGY OF THE CRITICAL: PAULO FREIRE

As interest in critical literacy has grown over the past few decades, to varying effects, in different parts of the world, a relevant and appropriately critical question is, Whose theories and perspectives are informing critical literacy? As with other large theoretical frameworks available to support our thinking about learning and cognition, **critical theory** has several historical trajectories, situated meanings, and manifestations.

When critical literacy is conceptualized as the active and often resistant engagement with texts, it is derived from and genealogically linked to the work of Paulo Freire, the Brazilian philosopher, activist, and educator. Freire, through his work with adult literacy campaigns and efforts in Brazil, brought to bear education as a site for emancipation, empowerment, and social justice. Born and raised in low socioeconomic conditions, Freire earned recognition, acclaim, and even controversial attention for the emancipatory literacy education he conducted with adults in poverty-stricken areas of Brazil. He worked with adults to counter forces that kept them intellectually, culturally, and politically disempowered, and he did it through literacy education. Freire's 1987 book with Donaldo Macedo cast a view of literacy as cultural politics. That is, literacy training should not only provide reading, writing, and numeracy, but it should be considered "a set of practices that functions to either empower or disempower people" (p. 187). Literacy should at all times be analyzed according to whether it serves to "reproduce existing social formations or serves as a set of cultural practices that promote democratic and emancipatory change" (p. viii). Literacy as cultural politics is also related in Freire's work in emancipatory theory and critical theory of society. Hence, emancipatory literacy "becomes a vehicle by which the oppressed are equipped with the necessary tools to reappropriate their history, culture, and language practices" (p. 159).

This view of literacy as a tool, process, and product that serves to empower those traditionally held outside of powerful positions, both informal and formal, is what informs the exploration of critical literacy in this book. We subscribe to a view that all texts are representations and that the practice of literacy is potentially a tool for empowerment or disempowerment. In helping students to become literate subjects of the state, we view the ability to critique texts as equally essential as the ability to decode them.

DEFINING CRITICAL LITERACY

Freebody and Luke (1990) define critical literacy as one of four processes that readers should employ when encountering text. Along with the more familiar practices of code breaker (coding competence), meaning maker (semantic competence), and text user (pragmatic competence), we need to consider the practices of reader as text critic. While each of these four processes marks an area of what it means to be literate, and each has, to varying degrees, been part of literacy pedagogy and curriculum, far less attention has been paid to the fourth process, being a text critic. This fourth dimension forces us to explicitly discuss the ways in which text is mediated as a tool of institutional shaping of discourses and social practices. This positioning is quite different from the traditional stance that text occupies in American educational and political discourse. Typically, texts, namely print-based books, are glorified as gateways to other worlds, keepers of stores of knowledge, and inanimate confidants and friends. In this way, texts are innocuous sources of information and wisdom. And while we can all think of certain texts that have performed those functions for us, to treat reading education in this sole manner belies the highly dialogic nature of classrooms, in which interactions shape knowledge, power, and discourse (Fairclough, 1989). Narrowly defined views of reading also deny the pervasive role that text, both print and visual, plays in shaping our identities, resources, and opportunities (Luke & Freebody, 1999). All four processes, as named by Luke and Freebody, work in conjunction, but the role of critically analyzing and transforming texts is one that is rarely sanctioned in school settings. Helping students to assume critical stances toward texts means supporting them in questioning the voices behind texts, who is represented and who is not, and what positions texts are assuming.

It is important to note that when we are talking about critical literacy, we make a distinction between its philosophical orientation and that of **critical reading**. Critical reading, arising from the liberal-humanist philosophical tradition, emphasizes such skill-based tasks as distinguishing fact from opinion and, at a more advanced level, recognizing propaganda in texts (Cervetti, Damico, & Pardeles, 2001). At that more advanced level, critical reading begins to edge in the direction of critical literacy, but it is still rooted in a Rationalist view of the world (Cervetti et al., 2001). That is, critical reading rests on the fundamental view expressed by Descartes and others that "knowledge of the world can be attained through reason, that this knowledge is universal and deductive in character, and that everything is fundamentally explainable by this universal system" (Cervetti et al., 2001, p. 4). In essence, meaning resides in texts to be deduced through careful, thoughtful exegesis.

In contrast, critical literacy views text meaning making as a process of construction with a particularly critical eye toward elements of the particular historical, social, and political contexts that permeate and foreground any text. Because critical literacy has its roots in critical pedagogy and therefore in Freirian and neo-Marxist approaches to social theory (Burbules & Berk, 1999), questions about power, privilege, and oppression are paramount. Thus, the reader is always looking behind the text to identify its hidden agendas, power groups with an interest in its message, and a recognition that all texts are ideological (Cervetti et al., 2001). When readers take this stance, they develop a critical consciousness, fostering a search for justice and equity by reading the meanings behind the text. Questions about whose version of history is sanctioned, whose energy policy is supported by a text, or how the reader or characters in a novel are positioned by an author all fall within the realm of critical literacy. Indeed, these questions go well beyond a techno-rational critical reading stance. In essence, engaging in critical reading is a search for a verifiable reading, whereas critical literacy is the endeavor to work within multiple plausible interpretations of a text.

In an era of mass consumerism and fast capitalism (New London Group, 1999), critical literacy offers a balance point to counter hegemonic forces and simple solutions to complex issues. Most important, it places students and teachers in a questioning frame of mind that moves beyond didactic, factual learning. In fact, some researchers have found that it is with exactly those most marginalized students that critical pedagogy is able to be taken up readily and passionately (Morrell & Duncan-Andrade, 2002). Projects such as UCLA's youth participatory action research projects demonstrate how posing questions of representation and power are easily taken up by those who have experiential knowledge as outsiders to cultural, political, and economic capital.

Several studies have begun to surface in the United States in the past few years that explore potential uses of critical literacy in classrooms (Alvermann, Moon, & Hagood, 1999; Lewis & Fabos, 2000; Stevens, 2001; Tobin, 2000; Young, 2000). Typically, these studies have drawn from popular culture texts to engage students' interests in exploring critical literacy roles. For example, Margaret Hagood (Alvermann et al., 1999) explored children's discussions as they explained why they shaped their self-created superheroes in certain ways and what visual images they used to depict traits such as gender, power, and personality. In another classroom, students shared examples of popular culture and explored questions of who was represented, who was not represented, what aspects of American society were reflected in the popular culture, and who stood to benefit or be hurt by the images (Stevens, 2001).

While this handful of studies sheds light on the great potential for critical literacy practices to create space for children's complex interpretations of media texts, few studies have explored this potentiality with texts more typically sanctioned in school settings. In fact, authors like Hagood (Alvermann et al., 1999) have drawn cautionary lines about the very real and often actualized danger of infringement upon students' **fandoms** from adultist perspectives. In addition to this caution, we also aver that a dominant association with critical literacy and popular culture texts implicitly promotes school-sanctioned texts as bias-free or not in need of critical inquiry. This very practice undermines one of the basic tenets of critical theory—that power, privilege, and oppression are inherent characteristics in all socially mediated contexts. In other words, all texts have biases, from the vibrant, polished videos on MTV, to the seemingly more innocent textbooks that are familiar to primary and secondary classrooms.

In the next section, we explore a classroom scenario in which the same types of questions are posed to a school-sanctioned text. This fictional scenario is based on the authors' experiences with a few science teachers who have used critical literacy activities in their classrooms.

MRS. CUTTER'S CLASS

As the students filter into Mrs. Cutter's fifth-grade classroom, they notice the large, unwieldy science textbooks on their desks. A few students groan as they suspect another session of round-robin reading, as they are accustomed to this common practice when working with textbooks. While this textbook, *Scott Foresman Science* (Cooney et al., 2000), features the bright colors, bold headings, and graphics suggested by content area literacy researchers (e.g., Alvermann & Phelps, 1998), the students do not seem to be any more enraptured by its content. To set the stage for today's lesson and topic, Mrs. Cutter asks students to spend a few minutes freewriting about the recent energy crises that have been occupying the nation's headlines. During a whole class sharing session, several students offer what they recall of the news items.

Jeremy offers, "The news shows are all talking like we're going to run out soon."

Kirsten adds, "I heard from my cousin in California that her lights went out last week. They do it to save electricity for later."

After a few more students share some of their thoughts, Mrs. Cutter asks them to open their books to pages B134 and B135, which contain information about how electricity is siphoned to consumers. She asks Justin to read aloud the first paragraph. He reads the following section:

Different sources of energy can be used to turn a generator's drive shaft and produce electricity. Notice in each of the pictures below that the generator's drive shaft attaches to a turbine. Like a pinwheel that spins when air rushes past it, each turbine below spins as steam or water moves through it. This spins the drive shaft. The drive shaft turns a magnet inside a coil of wire in the generator. Electricity is produced. (p. B134)

After Justin has finished reading, Mrs. Cutter asks Jacwelin to read the next paragraph:

A few power plants use tides or waves as their energy source. Modern windmills, such as those to the right, use wind energy to spin built-in generators. Altogether, generators produce almost all the electricity people use. Some devices produce electricity without a generator. Batteries change chemical energy directly into electrical energy. Special solar panels change light energy directly into electrical energy. (p. B135)

Mrs. Cutter then asks students to use the reading to answer the following questions that she displays using the overhead projector: (a) Who runs the power plants? (b) Who receives the electricity? (c) Is the electricity distributed in equal quantities? (d) How much does the electricity cost? and (e) What are all the possible alternative sources of energy?

After the students struggle with the questions for a few moments, Eric raises his hand and tells Mrs. Cutter that it doesn't seem like the answers to the questions can be found in the book.

"Great point, Eric. I knew that when I gave you guys the questions. Do you think that these are still good questions to pursue?" Mrs. Cutter asks. She leads the students in a discussion of the gap between the book's representation of electricity production and consumption and the realities of the current energy crisis. Mrs. Cutter then gives them the assignment for the day: to research how the information about electricity and energy should be written and to rewrite the passages in the textbook. Students work individually, in pairs, and small groups and use the textbook, trade books, and current periodicals on the Internet to investigate issues related to electricity.

At one point during the day, one group of students approaches Mrs. Cutter to ask if they can change the focus of their project to nuclear energy. When Mrs. Cutter inquires about the need to switch, the students point out the textbook's authors only devoted three to four paragraphs to nuclear energy, whereas other energy sources received three to four pages' worth of explanation and diagrams. Mrs. Cutter compliments the group on their critical reading of the text and encourages them in their newly defined project.

By the end of the day, most students are ready to share their writings. Before sharing their paragraph, Justin and his peers explain that they tried to rewrite the sentences so that the reader could tell who were the active agents. For example, the sentence that read "Electricity is produced" has been changed to "Public and private companies produce electricity and sell it to people for a profit."

Another group has constructed a list of pros and cons of using windmills as a power source. They cite the role of climate and the dominance of generators as obstacles to increased use of alternative sources of producing electricity.

At the end of the sharing session, Mrs. Cutter asks the students if they like their versions better than the textbook's. Most students nod to indicate that they like the revised versions better. Mrs. Cutter then asks the students if these versions could appear in a textbook. The students are not quite as collectively sure about this question. Some of the students maintain that the versions could be used, while others state that textbooks should stick to the facts. Mrs. Cutter asks the students to consider whether any of their versions used anything other than facts.

"No," Chelsea clarifies, "it's just that you could tell what we thought."

"And you couldn't tell what the textbook authors thought from their writing?" Mrs. Cutter asks.

"No, I don't think so," Chelsea concludes.

"Maybe they just think that electricity is given equally to everyone," suggests Justin.

"Maybe," Mrs. Cutter says. "Is that the opinion that they'd like you to form?"

The class continues to discuss the intentions of the textbook's authors.

The preceding scenario highlights a possible situation in which students read for a purpose, construct meaning, and also assume critical stances toward a seemingly innocuous text. Conducting lessons that foster critical literacy requires that teachers explicitly confront their own beliefs and assumptions about the role of activities, discourse, and power within classrooms. Teachers must also be prepared to provide space for students to express the complex ways in which we respond to texts (Tobin, 2000). To assume that students are innocent dupes at the mercy of print and media texts is to also effectively silence their voices. The issues raised by critical literacy as a component of literacy pedagogy are complex, to say the least. They are also, however, apropos in today's fast-paced, text-saturated, media-driven worlds.

PROBLEMATIZING CLASSROOM APPLICATIONS OF CRITICAL LITERACY

In this scenario, Mrs. Cutter provides guidance by acting as a sort of mediator between the text and her students as they construct comprehension and assume critical stances. This role is a common classroom application of critical literacy (Gilbert, 1993), as is providing multiple texts and using questions to raise issues of power and agency. However, this role is far from simplistic. As many authors have discussed, teachers who employ critical literacy questions and discussions with their students must wrestle with the complexities of opening the possibilities to alternative readings and meanings (e.g., Comber, 1993; Gilbert, 1993). Teachers may find themselves replacing the hegemonic positioning of traditional readings with their preferred reading. For example, would a feminist teacher be open to a student's masculine reading of a popular culture advertisement? On what bases could teachers decide that the construction of their critical comprehension was critical enough? In this sense, there is room for critical literacy to be interrogated by the rationalist principles of critical reading and thinking.

Another key aspect of critical literacy in the classroom is the question of which texts to use. As Gilbert (1993) posed, "How, for instance, can students learn about the social context of language, unless they are able to experience the impact of actual language practices in contexts that are of interest and concern to them?" (p. 76). Questions such as these underscore the need for critical literacy practices to be reformulated and adapted according to specific contexts, purposes, and participants. And while the endeavor of using critical literacy in the classroom is not without complication, it is also clear that its very complexities are the reasons why it should be pursued. Texts are used for various purposes and to varying degrees of success in today's fast, text-saturated economy. It is no longer appropriate for classroom discussions of text to assume that all literacy forms are innocuous and equal in their use of power and agency. In a democratic society, it is imperative that we critique texts with the rigor that will empower our students to be proficient, purposeful, and savvy consumers and producers of text.

DISCUSSION QUESTIONS

For teachers who are embarking on the use of critical literacy in the classroom, a logical segue is through questioning, one of the most powerful scaffolding and modeling tools teachers can employ in the classroom. As a starting point to building critical literacy into comprehension activities, consider the examples below of these types of questions and inquiry points. Choose a text and address your reading of this text with these questions. With other participants, you might discuss the various interpretations and their plausibility:

- Who/what is represented in this text?
- Who/what is absent or not represented?
- What is the author trying to accomplish with this text?
- For whom was this text written?
- Who stands to benefit/be hurt from this text?
- How is language used in specific ways to convey ideas in this text?
- How do other texts/authors represent this idea?
- How could this text be rewritten to convey a different idea/representation?

KEY TERMS FROM THIS CHAPTER

Critical literacy: active questioning of the stance found within, behind, and among texts. Critical literacy is an emancipatory endeavor, supporting students to ask regular questions about representation, benefit, marginalization, and interests.

Critical theory: a broad epistemic framework that can be found in many fields in the social sciences and humanities. Generally, these arenas share in common a critique of dominance, a commitment to emancipation, and the use of critique and reflection as means to empowerment.

RECOMMENDED FURTHER READING

Critical Literacy

Fehring, H., & Green, P. (Eds.). (2001). *Critical literacy: A collection of articles from the Australian Literacy Educators' Association*. Newark, DE: International Reading Association.

Freire, P. (2000). *Pedagogy of the oppressed* (30th anniversary ed.). New York: Continuum Press.

Luke, A. (2000). Critical literacy in Australia: A matter of context and standpoint. *Journal of Adolescent & Adult Literacy, 43*, 448–461.

Luke, A., & Freebody, P. (1999). Further notes on the four resources model. *Reading Online* [Live chat]. Retrieved from www.readingonline.org

Classroom Implications of Critical Literacy in the United States

Alvermann, D. E., Moon, J. S., & Hagood, M. C. (1999). *Popular culture in the classroom: Teaching and researching critical media literacy*. Newark, DE: International Reading Association.

Bean, T. W., & Moni, K. (2003). Developing students' critical literacy: Exploring identity construction in young adult fiction. *Journal of Adolescent & Adult Literacy, 46*, 638–648.

Leland, C., Harste, J., Ociepka, A., Lewison, M., & Vasquez, V. (1999). Talking about books. Exploring critical literacy: You can hear a pin drop. *Language Arts, 77*(1), 70–77.

Stevens, L. P. (2001). *South Park* and society: Curricular implications of popular culture in the classroom. *Journal of Adolescent & Adult Literacy, 44*, 548–555.

Tobin, J. (2000). *"Good guys don't wear hats": Children's talk about the media*. New York: Teachers College Press.

Discourse Analysis

Fairclough, N. (1989). *Language and power*. New York: Longman.

Fairclough, N. (1995). *Critical discourse analysis: The critical study of language*. New York: Longman.

Gee, J. (1999). *Discourse analysis*. New York: Routledge.

Halliday, M. A. K. (1994). *An introduction to functional grammar* (2nd ed.). London: Edward Arnold.

REFERENCES

Alvermann, D. E., & Phelps, S. F. (1998). *Content reading and literacy: Succeeding in today's diverse classrooms*. Boston: Allyn & Bacon.

Alvermann, D. E., Moon, J. S., & Hagood, M. C. (1999). *Popular culture in the classroom: Teaching and researching critical media literacy*. Newark, DE: International Reading Association.

Bean, T. W. (2001). An update on reading in the content areas. *Reading Online*. Retrieved from www.readingonline.org

Burbules, N., & Berk, R. (1999). Critical thinking and critical pedagogy: Relations, differences, and limits. In T. S. Popkewitz & L. Fendler (Eds.), *Critical theories in education: Changing terrains of knowledge and politics*. New York: Routledge.

Cervetti, G., Damico, J. S., & Pardeles, M. J. (2001). A tale of differences: Comparing the traditions, perspectives, and educational goals of critical reading and critical literacy. *Reading Online*. Retrieved from www.readingonline.org

Comber, B. (1993). Classroom expectations in critical literacy. *Australian Journal of Language and Literacy, 16*(1), 90–102.

Cooney, T., DiSpezio, M. A., Foots, B., Matamoros, A. L., Nyquist, K. B., & Ostlund, K. L. (2000). *Scott Foresman science*. Glenview, IL: Addison Wesley.

Fairclough, N. (1989). *Language and power*. New York: Longman.

Freebody, P., & Luke, A. (1990) Literacies programs: Debates and demands in cultural context: *Prospect: Australian Journal of TESOL, 5*(7), 7–16.

Freire, P. (1970). *Pedagogy of the oppressed*. New York: Seabury Press.

Freire, P., & Macedo, D. (1987). *Literacy: Reading the word and the world*. Westport, CT: Bergin & Garvey.

Gee, J. P. (1996). *Social linguistics and literacies: Ideology in discourses* (2nd ed.). Bristol, PA: Taylor & Francis.

Gilbert, P. (1993). (Sub)versions: Using sexist language practices to explore critical literacy. *Australian Journal of Language and Literacy, 16*(4), 75–83.

Heath, S. B. (1983). *Ways with words: Language, life, and work in communities and classrooms*. Cambridge, UK: Cambridge University Press.

Lewis, C. (2002). *Literary practices as social acts: Power, status, and cultural norms in the classroom*. Mahwah, NJ: Lawrence Erlbaum.

Lewis, C., & Fabos, B. (2000). But will it work in the heartland? A response and illustration. *Journal of Adolescent & Adult Literacy, 43*, 462–469.

Luke, A., & Freebody, P. (1999). Further notes on the four resources model. *Reading Online*. Retrieved from www.readingonline.org

Luke, A., & Luke, C. (2001). Adolescence lost/childhood regained: On early intervention and the emergence of the techno-subject. *Journal of Early Childhood Literacy, 1*(1), 91–120.

Michaels, S. (1981). "Sharing time": Children's narrative styles and differential access to literacy. *Language in Society, 10,* 423–442.

Moje, E. (2000). *All the stories we have: Adolescents' insights about literacy and learning in secondary schools.* Newark, DE: International Reading Association.

Moore, D. W., Bean, T. W., Birdyshaw, D., & Rycik, J. A. (1999). Adolescent literacy: A position statement. *Journal of Adolescent & Adult Literacy, 43,* 97–112.

Morrell, E., & Duncan-Andrade, J. (2002). Promoting academic literacy with urban youth through engaging hip-hop culture. *English Journal, 85,* 88–92.

New London Group (1999). A pedagogy of multiliteracies: Designing social futures. *Harvard Educational Review, 66*(1), 60–92.

Stevens, L. P. (2001). *South Park* and society: Instructional and curricular implications of popular culture in the classroom. *Journal of Adolescent & Adult Literacy, 44,* 548–555.

Tobin, J. (2000). *The good guys don't wear hats: Children's talk about the media.* New York: Teachers College Press.

Young, J. P. (2000). Boy talk: Critical literacy and masculinities. *Reading Research Quarterly, 35*(3), 312–337.

CHAPTER 2

Why We Need Critical Literacy

Dynamic Texts and Identity Formation

In this chapter we unpack two of the most compelling aspects of literacy and culture: the shifting role of texts in today's marketplaces and how we interact with texts to form our identities. We begin with a vignette that illustrates the dynamic nature of contemporary texts and their role in students' various in- and out-of-school identities. The proliferation of texts available on the Internet and other multimedia displays suggests an increasing need for critical literacy practices.

It is about 4:30 on Wednesday afternoon, and ninth graders Samantha and Jordyn are hanging out after school at Jordyn's house, enjoying time away from the watchful eyes of their parents and teachers. They are in Jordyn's room and have been surfing the Net without any particular purpose. They spend a few minutes IMing[1] other friends who are similarly spending time after school. Then they log on to the Web site of a popular teen magazine for girls, *Young Miss*.[2] As the Web site loads, Samantha closes several pop-up windows that contain advertisements for the magazine, cosmetics, and clothing lines. She chooses to leave open a pop-up window for clothes from Abercrombie & Fitch, one of the girls' favorite stores. They browse at the online special for a few minutes and then return to the *Young Miss* Web site.

> *Samantha:* Hey, look! They have a new quiz online today. It will tell you if you are more of a Britney [Spears], a Christina [Aguilera], or a Mandy [Moore]. Do you want to take it?
>
> *Jordyn:* Nah, you go ahead.
>
> *Samantha:* OK, let's see here.

As Samantha navigates her way through each of the four screens that asks her a series of multiple-choice questions, she and Jordyn vacillate between taking the questions seriously and poking fun at the quiz.

> *Samantha:* OK, next question. On a first date, would you rather (a) have a nice dinner with your parents and potential boyfriend—yeah, right! (b) sneak out after your parents have gone to bed to go clubbing, or (c) both (a) and (b).
>
> *Jordyn:* OK, so all the A's are Britney answers and the B's are Christina?
>
> *Samantha:* I'm not sure. I think the A's are Mandy, like all prissy and Goody Two-shoes. The B's are Christina, like right to the point, slutty kind of . . .
>
> *Jordyn:* [interrupting] Yeah, that's it!
>
> *Samantha:* And the C's are Britney. All sweetness and innocence outside but a little nasty on the inside.
>
> *Jordyn:* OK, so what's your score?
>
> *Samantha:* I scored 25 on the Britney—can you believe that?!
>
> *Jordyn:* [laughing] Oh, yeah, that's you, totally. They nailed you!

While Samantha's and Jordyn's teachers and parents might dismiss their after-school Web surfing as little more than killing time, the girls have actually engaged in a fairly sophisticated series of literacy practices. Amid these events are congruent and overlapping issues of expanded definitions of text, wider examples of **text genres**, and active negotiation and performance of identity.

LITERACY PROFICIENCY AND
NEW TEXTS: A MOVING TARGET

As we discussed in Chapter 1, one of the key reasons why critical literacy should occupy a central position in literacy education is the overwhelming nature and amount of text in today's world. Without the ability to negotiate and critically examine multiple forms of text, a "proficient" reader might only be proficient enough to superficially understand these **texts**. Different from reading between the lines, reading inferentially, or the oft-touted "higher-order thinking skills," critical literacy demands reading texts and filtering them for positionalities, agendas, and purposes. In such explorations of text, we should expect to hear dissenting opinions, many plausible interpretations, and discussions of the larger social, historical, cultural, and political contexts. For an example of such a critical discussion, review the textbook-based critical literacy approach provided in Chapter 1. Schooling has tended, in its use of textbooks and other print-based texts, to privilege superficial, factual-level comprehension while leaving questions of power and representation unexplored.

Typically, texts that are sanctioned in schools and used to promote students' literacy levels are fairly similar in format and presentation. They are printed on paper and follow linear formats, with either a fiction sequence of plot development or a nonfiction organization of facts and details. In both of these types of text, explicit text genres, or identifiable patterns of text, can be labeled. In fact, identification of text genres such as compare/contrast, main idea/detail, and the five-act play has been taught explicitly to students since the 1980s as part of **content area literacy** and secondary English curricula (e.g., Readence, Bean, & Baldwin, 2004). While these types of activities are valuable, they are not sufficient in being literate with **digitally mediated texts**, which might well be organized nonlinearly. In addition, the kinds of texts we now encounter in an information age, both through sheer volume and varying formats, demand sharper uses of critical lenses. In fact, considering recent research on students' efforts to navigate digital texts of various forms on the Internet, McNabb (2006), studying middle-level students' Internet needs, noted: "Reading hypertext is a different experience than reading linear print" (p. 20). In particular, navigating digital text departs dramatically from more linear-established text patterns of organization. Students must negotiate bundled masses of text through layers of links that may be idiosyncratic to the Web site's creator. More important for critical literacy, students need instruction and scaffolding in critical literacy stances precisely because Internet sites vary in authenticity, biases, and accurate information. McNabb suggested: "Many of today's middle-level classrooms were designed to prepare students with the literacy skills needed in nonnetworked cultures of the 20th century" (p. 122).

The texts that Samantha and Jordyn negotiated in the few minutes of their surfing hardly fit within the typical texts found in schools, particularly economically disadvantaged schools. Instead of using paper, Samantha and Jordyn solely negotiated electronic texts, including words, moving and still images, and sounds. They identified several different text genres, including the pop-up advertisements and the format and sequence of an online quiz to determine personality. They moved deftly between texts, breaking linear progression of activity, and adequately sifting through dynamic organization of the Web site's links, features, and associated texts. They certainly were reading, but it would not look similar to the kind of reading that they might do sitting with a single textbook.

The essence of any definition of literacy is meaning. We read, write, talk, and listen in order to understand and to be understood, in myriad ways. While this focus on the processes and skills involved in deriving and projecting meaning through text has remained constant, the contexts and tasks of literacy have morphed, expanded, and proliferated rapidly recently. In addition to the printed and oral word, images are intertwined with text, in relentless fashion. Hypertext, e-books, pop-up boxes, streaming video, instant messaging, cell phones, smart phones that mimic larger devices like laptop computers, digital music devices, pagers, digital video recorders, personal desk assistants (PDAs), and video games are but a few of the tools that have left their mark on shifting and burgeoning definitions of text.

Numerous Web sites, including Myspace.com, Facebook.com, as well as popular reality television shows like *Survivor, Lost*, and *Real World TV*, offer sites for critique and are in marked contrast to more traditional forms of narrative. Each of these sites positions people in a fashion open to critique around gender, ethnic, and socioeconomic issues, to mention a few. Thus, all forms of text, including digital, film, and television productions, can be powerful sites for the practice of critical literacy.

In addition to the processes and skills of literacy, we must now also think about practices, that is to say, what the particular literacy event is and how the parameters and context of that event play a role in how we use literacy skills and processes to decode, comprehend, and critique texts (Gee, 1996; McNabb, 2006). To be literate means being able to engage in a range of literacy practices, drawing upon different sets of skills and processes suited to those particular practices.

The consideration of literacy practices helps to underscore the need to be a critical reader. For example, if you approached reading your daily mail with the same detail and attention that you use following directions to hook up your new computer, you would quickly find yourself obeying advertisements demanding immediate responses to take advantage of low-interest mortgage rates. Being able to negotiate contexts that involve digital literacies and tools such as computers, PDAs, smartphones, and interactive television is not a simple matter of following a linear progression of decoding and factual comprehension skills. Rather, the need to be a critical reader of the bombardment of text, in all its various and dynamic forms, is at an unprecedented high. Samantha and Jordyn deftly screened and dismissed the various pop-up advertisements screaming for their attention. They critically chose to pay attention to one that resonated with their preferences and deleted the rest. Furthermore, Samantha and Jordyn were able to shuttle between mocking the text genre and predictability of the online quiz and taking up certain aspects that defined them in certain ways as young American girls. Their textual practice reflects a complex weaving of purpose, tone, and readers' approach.

However, at the same time, Samantha and Jordyn are clearly regular visitors of the teen magazine's Web site. In what ways do their regular visits to this Web site reinforce media-sanctioned ideas that the optimal image of a female teenager is skinny, Caucasian, and endlessly happy? To what extent are the regular visits to the Abercrombie & Fitch Web site reinforcing overly thin ideals of the human body, exposing these young girls to a site critiqued for its hypersexuality and latent racism (Moje & Van Helden, 2004)?

These are complicated questions, and our exploration of them is not without ethical considerations of impinging on the fandom pleasure that Samantha and Jordyn gain from them and also not assuming Samantha and Jordyn to be guileless innocents, capable of facile following. However, what we can tell from this brief scenario is that text, meaning, and context are at the heart of Samantha's and Jordyn's literacy events. Clearly, this is not the type of literacy event we would likely encounter in a school setting. In that sense, literacies, how we interact with text, are plural. At times, using the dominant discourse found in mainstream news shows is appropriate, whereas other situations would call for completely different patterns of interaction and content. How we learn to modify our literacy skills and processes to the practice at hand is through engaging in a variety of literacy practices. Samantha and Jordyn are arguably multiliterate readers, able to demonstrate proficiency in linear and nonlinear literacy practices, but these proficiencies have been developed through access to a variety of literacy practices. The demands of a global networked culture far exceed the old literacies and expectations for reading and comprehending static texts (McNabb, 2006). Critical literacy is imperative, but clearly, access to advanced technology influences students' experience and success with deconstructing nonnetworked and nontraditional text forms. Samantha and Jordyn are fortunate to have access to digitally mediated literacies, but the same cannot be said for all the students in the United States (McNabb, 2006). Not being able to negotiate heightened and diverse literacies will certainly prevent our students from accessing a full array of life choices.

Schools must begin to reflect expanded definitions of both text and literacies to more closely reflect the multiple literacies used in contexts outside of classrooms. Currently, most of our classrooms more strongly reflect the technology and texts of the 1950s rather than contemporary texts that are hybridized across format and purpose. Furthermore, a few recent studies (Hagood, 2002; Hagood, Stevens, & Reinking, 2002; McNabb, 2006) indicate that the ways in which we interact with printed texts (e.g., the reading and writing processes as traditionally taught as a sequence of a handful of steps) are not the same or even transferable to those literacy practices with digitally mediated texts.

Transforming the very texts we use in schools is a first step to reconsidering the processes, skills, and practices that fall under the large umbrellas of reading and literacy. By increasing the types, formats, and text genres included in schools, we will also be changing and expanding the textual practices traditionally sanctioned in school spaces. Increasing the amount and type of texts is a companion characteristic to engaging students in critical literacy. While critique can be engaged with a single text, being a text critic can also be enacted through the comparison and juxtaposition of differing texts. In keeping with a reconsideration of the skills and processes demanded in today's information age, a reconceptualization of what kinds of texts should be included is similarly timely and relevant. Just as the landscape of texts has changed, so too must our work in it.

Now that we have laid the foundation for understanding how the nature, format, amount, and genre of texts and textual practices have changed and require a more critical approach to literacy, we turn our attention to theoretical reasons why critical literacy is crucial. In addition to our contextual need to be skilled readers and writers, critical literacy also arises from the nature of texts as attention seekers and tools of **identity formation**. In the next section of this chapter, we raise still more complex issues of how texts interact with our attention and the intricate ways that identity construction is wrapped up in texts and literacy practices.

TEXTS, ATTENTION, AND IDENTITY?

You are sitting in the airport terminal, waiting to board your flight and people watching as the minutes tick by. As you glance around the terminal, you notice one middle-aged woman glancing at the tourist products displayed, wearing a sweatshirt saying, "Grandmas rule." A young man walks by swiftly in his Ralph Lauren suit, talking into the earpiece of his Sprint cell phone while checking his Palm pilot PDA for his itinerary that day. A teenaged girl ambles by, listening to her iPod and adjusting her FUBU sweatshirt. All of these people have chosen particular items of clothing that work as textual markers of who they are. No doubt, just as the middle-aged woman was browsing through the coffee cups that used southwestern art to loudly proclaim "San Antonio!," they all, as you have, chosen brands, clothing, and other texts that have first captured their attention and reflected their senses of self. Simply put, they have chosen certain attention-garnering texts that resonate with their identities.

We argue that this understanding of information, text, and attention should be at the forefront of our thinking and pedagogical planning for literacy, along with a strong foundation in understanding contemporary identity theories. Critical literacy becomes crucial in contemporary culture, in part, because of the "[m]edia culture of spectacle that has normalized the notion that entertainment is news and news is entertainment" (Goodman, 2003, p. 6). In essence, a multitude of "texts," many of them visual in nature and grappling for our attention via flashy colors and movement, cry out for **deconstruction** and critique. In teaching students the art of deconstruction, we open the world to critique and thoughtful examination. "Deconstruction turns a text against itself, multiplying its meanings" (Lynn, 2001, p. 97). But why, given the rapid pace of our lives and those of our students, should we take the time to slow down and notice both the form and function of the texts that enter our lives?

THE TRANSFORMATION OF TEXTS AND READERS' ATTENTION

A great deal of attention has been devoted to compelling us to prepare students for the information age and today's knowledge-based economy, but, as educators, we need to better understand and conceptualize how this information age uses texts. A useful framework for our consideration is Goldhaber's notion of an **attention economy** (as cited in Lankshear & Knobel, 2002, p. 1). Critical theorists Lankshear and Knobel have applied this sociological concept to digitally mediated literacies, and it is useful here as a way of understanding how texts work and to what purposes in an information age. Within this theory, we are, as consumers and potential buyers, first bombarded by images that seek to gain, keep, and direct our attention to particular purchases, often through digitally mediated modes and effects. To get us to purchase a good, service, or commodity, advertisers, companies, and even public agencies use print and digital texts to gain our attention. While this has arguably been the case for the duration of advertising, what makes it an economic system is the volume of texts competing with each other to first gain this attention.

While we realize we are bombarded with information via conventional texts, the Internet, media saturation, billboards, electronic billboards, and a host of other older communications means (e.g., skywriting and small planes towing banners), these media are strangely ignored in policy conversations about what counts as literacy proficiencies. Some thinkers believe this is a huge gap in our literacy curriculum and pedagogy. Estimates suggest that we and our students spend somewhere in the vicinity of 60% of our waking hours consuming media in some form (Lankshear & Knobel, 2002). Television, film, recordings, and the Internet rank at the top of this consumption list, but we can be sure that newer media yet to hit the scene will be vying for our attention as well. The media-driven charisma of star power and their fans (often our students) consumes a significant portion of the information economy and celebrity-conscious culture. While information is in large supply, human attention, and its associated monetary resources, is limited. Thus, an endless array of display devices, including computerized jackets with digitized images and messages, attention-grabbing pop art, outrageous Super Bowl media spots, and even journalism that uses fear headlines, jar us into paying attention to their messages.

The attention economy is fueled by attempts at ever-greater originality and provocation in design and display of texts and images (Lankshear & Knobel, 2002). Privacy is often replaced in this fluid, Internet, and media-based medium with identities forged through sharing one's thoughts and experiences. Sharing minicam video images, voice recordings, blogs, interviews, podcasts, and auto-biographical information is now the norm, offering even the most mundane individuals a forum for their ideas via chat rooms and interest groups. While the detailed debates about a textually mediated celebrity culture are outside the scope of this book, we bring up these images to show the dissonance between contemporary literacy policies and practices and the textual practices found in other social spaces. While we are not necessarily advocating that reality shows become the new fad in curriculum design, we are suggesting that educational policy and practice would do well to consider the skills, process, and practices needed by our students to mediate current and future lifeworlds.

With rare exceptions (e.g., Alvermann, Moon, & Hagood, 1999; Goodman, 2003; Kist, 2005; Stevens, 2001), curriculum planning in the United States has remained firmly rooted in an older era of traditional texts, low-level comprehension questions, and narrow assessments. Not surprisingly, the fast-moving worlds of business and advertising have devoted significant resources to designing and purchasing media spots that acknowledge consumers' limited economies of attention.

Clothing ads aimed at middle-class, suburban teens typically feature rail-thin males and females with blond hair. These images weigh in peoples' views of acceptable and unacceptable identities. Staying in the flow in a consumer society means having the right clothes and looking the part that goes with the clothes. In essence, ads are texts, constructed and aimed specifically at a particular demographic. They work in conjunction with other texts to provide us with options for performing ourselves, our identities. In this way, texts act as constitutive forces, creating and enacting possibilities for ways of being, doing, and acting. Of course, the problem with solely relying upon and/or critically taking up such texts is that there are capitalist interests behind these texts, and their goal is profit, not personal fulfillment, **agency**, or social justice. As an alternative to passive consumption of consumer-driven texts, students in some high school settings have undertaken the development of video documentaries and other media dealing with local issues and problems (Goodman, 2003; Kist, 2005). Topics center on critical community issues such as gun violence and gang affiliation. After-school programs offer space for innovative curricular efforts where creativity is less restricted. The audiences for this media-based student work moves beyond the narrower realm of the school site to include community leaders in positions where they can impact social change. In all cases, reading the world through the various forms of texts that students encounter becomes the launching pad for creative deconstruction and critique by students using videos, podcasts, music, and a host of other media.

Texts can and should be critically evaluated based on how they envision and position people in various roles, how we use them to construct aspects of our identity. Just as these advertisements work to persuade us to buy the sharpest and most compact high-definition television or sleekest refrigerator with brushed steel doors, they are constructing a certain kind of person, with a certain way of being, doing, and acting. In short, these texts, along with the other less overt but still commodified spaces of print-based texts, take up dialectic positions as we mediate our senses of ourselves, our identities. Within a world that is increasingly driven by corporations and economically based interests, the use of texts persuades us to buy but also offer potential discourses, or ways of being ourselves.

Given that all of us are potential consumers to be swayed by highly creative, shocking, and powerful media messages designed to get our attention, and ultimately to persuade us to purchase products, the need for critical literacy could not be more timely. Helping students develop well-honed critical filters to evaluate how they are being positioned by text messages and, equally important, how to design their own text messages is markedly absent from our systemic discussions of curriculum standards and assessments. In essence, this leaves schools and classrooms, particularly public schools in lower socioeconomic areas, in the role of creaking institutions badly out of sync with the information flow of new texts, transmitted globally and without conventional regard to the time and space constraints of traditional print-based texts.

Global markets, global manufacturers and purveyors of knowledge, and global consumers, already either horizontal in shape or lacking any physical shape at all, have arrived as new participants, stirring like a rising mist on a summer's morning round the soaring trunks of the trees in an old wood. They move inexorably across global space and time without respect to physical geography, political frontiers, or night and day. (Langhorne, 2001, p. 39)

Within the world of Web-based design, songs, icons, and catch statements compete to grab viewers' limited attention (Lankshear & Knobel, 2002). Arguably, the United States, with its overabundance of commercial space, both literal and figurative, may well offer more commercially based texts vying for consumers' attention than many other countries in the world. For example, the familiar Nike Swoosh works because of its simplicity and eye-catching design, along with numerous star performer associations like Tiger Woods. The use of virtually any surface to grab a potential customer's attention has become a commonplace advertising strategy. For example, if you purchase a cup of coffee in a coffee shop, you are likely to have a coffee sleeve advertising high-speed Internet connections in bright, eye-catching colors. It is no accident that large phone companies and cable television firms would view the clientele of suburban coffee shops as potential customers, given their willingness to plunk down something in the vicinity of $5 for a cup of coffee and milk. However, we tend to take these attention-grabbing devices for granted, rarely considering them "texts" for critical literacy discussions. If we are truly interested in developing an informed, aware, and critical citizenry, the variety of texts vying for our attention needs to become part of our curriculum design.

For example, having students collect attention-grabbing icons, ads, and multimedia forms of text from their neighborhood surroundings is one way to start developing their critical literacy. Although texts of all varieties need to be framed as representations (see Chapter 1 for a discussion of overemphasis on popular culture texts), tapping into texts of high interest may yield space for students to share their already existing critical literacy practices.

In addition, engaging students in creating their own digital and print-based designs that recognize how texts work to gain and maximize the attention of particular audiences moves the students into a high-level **metacognitive awareness** of how this form of text functions in the information age (Luke & Elkins, 1998). In fact, while it may seem at first that raising awarenesses of the potential impact of texts would be a disheartening venture, this is also what brings about agency.

In Chapter 4, we introduce various snapshots of classroom-based critical literacy practices aimed at engaging students at various levels in becoming conscious participants in critical literacy. Before moving to specific strategies, we want to continue situating our understandings of texts, the various elements of critical literacy, and one of the most important elements: the interaction between texts and identity formation.

TEXTS AS TOOLS OF IDENTITY FORMATION

In the past, through the fields of psychology and psychiatry, we have understood and theorized identity as basically internally contained. When peoples' personalities are discussed, they are often discussed in a way that connotes a static or constant feature to their personhood. For example, if we describe a man as being bossy, commanding, or statuesque, we don't often pause to think about how those features might only be performed and seem salient in relation to a particular context, with other participants, and interacting with particular kinds of texts.

Contemporary definitions of identity, however, reject unitary, simplistic notions of a static, autonomous self. Rather, our senses of identity contain two important aspects of fluidity. One, we shift how we act and behave from context to context. As we've mentioned, part and parcel of being a critical reader is being able to recognize the various discourses, or ways of being, doing, and acting (Gee, 1996) that are communicated via texts. Similarly and relationally, we shift our linguistic registers, behaviors, and tones when we move from context to context. Two, we use texts and textual markers as key ways of constructing and communicating our identities, particularly in relation to others. In the opening scenario, differing identities were suggested by the grandmother, the young businessman, and the teenager, all through use of textual markers.

We can think of identity as fluid and shifting based on contextual feedback and individual interpretation. That is, how we understand ourselves is, in large part, informed by where we find ourselves, with whom, and engaged in what practices. This is an important aspect of the classroom that often gets reduced to faculty room discussions of children and young adults from stereotypical stances. As a social context, the classroom is marked by participants interacting with each other, performing their senses of selves, and interpreting others' actions and practices. As we read texts together, we are engaged in **socially situated literacy practice**, with implications of identity construction and power. For example, in an in-depth ethnography of a fifth- and sixth-grade classroom, Lewis (2001) found that the teacher had a marked tendency to favor girls over boys in reader response discussions. The boys in class dealt with this inequity by acting out and viewing the reading discussions as manifestations of feminine literacy practice.

Texts, in a critical literacy-based classroom, become sites for explicit conversations that take into account our shifting identities and make students aware of potential imbalances in agency and voice. That is, who gets to speak and control the flow of discussion is problematic and worthy of consideration just as the content of what students say in a literature circle of nonfiction text discussion is also worthy of careful consideration. In this way, the participants in this classroom would discuss not only the content of the text but also how the text does its work, what language choices are made and why. This is what is known as **metalanguage**, or language about language. These conversations about metalanguage and discourse are crucial to aiding students to critically use texts as mediational tools—interactional tactics between themselves and the world around them.

One of the best ways to first develop this critical literacy stance and, ultimately, to infuse this perspective in your classroom is to adopt the practice of questioning texts in your own reading. Thus, when you pick up a magazine or newspaper, or watch television, consciously give some thought to who is not represented in these texts. In addition, who has voice and agency and who is silenced by this presentation? This is a crucial foundation for productive, critical citizenship in a democracy (Cherland & Harper, 2007; Harper & Bean, 2006).

Both texts and the classroom social contexts in which they are discussed become sites for critical literacy. Texts, from this viewpoint, are "cultural tools for establishing belongingness, identity, personhood, and ways of knowing" (Moje, Dillon, & O'Brien, 2000, p. 167). Figures in nonfiction accounts of history, as well as characters in novels, are depicted and positioned based on perceived identity, gender, ethnicity, and culture. "When fiction and non-fiction texts are carefully considered from a critical literacy perspective, silenced voices and marginalized groups come into sharper focus" (Stevens & Bean, 2003).

Multicultural literature offers a particularly powerful vehicle for incorporating critical literacy practices (Bean & Moni, 2003; Harper & Bean, 2006). For example, issues of democracy, freedom, equity, and social justice feature heavily in young adult and children's literature, and these works lend themselves to critical literacy questions and discussion. Award-winning young adult novels like Beverly Naidoo's (2000), *The Other Side of Truth,* about Sade and her family's exile from war-torn Nigeria to London deals with racism and social justice issues. Critical literacy questions concerning how Sade as a Nigerian is positioned in London go to the heart of understanding racist posturing. In addition, the novel deals with political coups, persecution of free speech, and a host of other issues. Numerous other young adult novels and children's literature selections can be found at the American Library Association Web site, as well as award-winning works listed each year by the International Reading Association at its Web site, along with resources through the National Council of Teachers of English and other organizations. Commercial bookstore sites and Amazon.com offer searchable collections of young adult and children's literature.

Activity: Take a look at Sharon Flake's (2001) award-winning young adult novel, *Money Hungry.*

The novel chronicles Raspberry, the main character's entrepreneurial spirit, driven largely by her desire to keep herself and her mother from becoming homeless. To do so, Raspberry sells items at school and, unbeknownst to her mom, amasses a substantial stash of cash in her bedroom. But the larger problem is her side business in school, which detracts from her work and, in one instance, results in students becoming ill after buying and eating old M&M's Raspberry sells to them. She gets into constant trouble with the school administration and her mom, but she is often operating out of fear after a bout of living on the street in an old car.

- How does the main character, Raspberry, construct her in-school identity in her middle school?
- How does the school principal position Raspberry when he meets with her?
- What systemic elements of society contribute to Raspberry's predicament?

TEXTS: MEDIATING IDENTITY AND CULTURE

When someone describes you as a soccer mom, gourmet cook, guitar player, artist, member of Generation X, or jogger, they have captured one tiny element of your identity. Similarly, if we describe a student as motivated, achievement oriented, lazy, or irresponsible, we have produced a limited, **essentialist label** that misses the complexity of any person's identity. In most contemporary discussions of identity, the social context and related discourse, coupled with an individual's subjective interpretation of others' language and actions, lead to a particular conception of the self within various contexts (Lewis, 2001). For example, a beginning surfer paddling out to Waikiki for the first time is potentially subject to ridicule if he or she inadvertently paddles in the way of an experienced surfer's ride on a wave. The experienced surfer, through language and gestures, positions the neophyte as an outsider, unworthy of membership in the advanced level of this sport. Back on the beach, our surfer is an accomplished symphonic musician, playing the cello in the local Honolulu Symphony, where being a hotshot surfer doesn't count. Thus, identity is intertwined with culture and the discourse of people performing in that culture. Identity from this standpoint is fluid and often contradictory (Lewis, 2001). Figure 2.1 displays the elements of identity as a dynamic process, heavily influenced by the social context and cultural dimensions of this context.

The culture of particular groups like surfers and symphonic musicians guides discourse in such a way that individuals come to regard themselves as insiders, outsiders, or actors temporarily getting by in an uncomfortable setting.

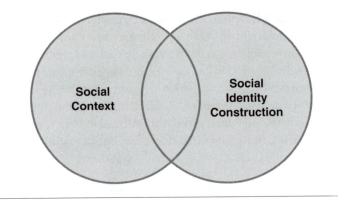

Figure 2.1   Identity as a Dynamic Process

When we consider identities to be social constructions, and therefore always open for change and conflict depending on the social interaction we find ourselves in, we open possibilities for rethinking the labels we so easily use to identify students. (McCarthey & Moje, 2002, p. 230)

In a similar fashion, Lewis (2001) defined culture as "a dynamic system within which social relations and identities are continuously negotiated and power is asymmetrical" (p. 12).

If the readings students encounter in the culture of the classroom are divorced from their experiences and interests, literacy becomes a school exercise to endure or resist. For example, Broughton and Fairbanks (2002) observed and interviewed Jessica, a sixth-grade Latina student in Texas. The classroom curriculum was heavily weighted toward passing the high-stakes state test in literacy. Jessica did not see any relationship between her journal writing and Internet reading at home and school learning. She was often bored in class and daydreamed to survive. The inclusion of multicultural literature that connected with Jessica's life would have enlivened her school experiences and, perhaps, caused her to forge a deeper connection with the classroom. Instead, she survived by feigning attention in sustained silent reading and making sure she appeared to the teacher to be "doing school" appropriately.

Viewing identity as a process rather than a unified category helps us look more closely at social practices in the classroom we often overlook (McCarthey, 2002). For example, small group and literature circle discussions are social contexts where discussions of texts are negotiated based upon gender and social power issues. This is an important element to consider, as we often assume that if we include high-interest books in a classroom, all will be well. Yet social context and asymmetrical power relations will ultimately determine how these books are discussed and how students regard themselves in this process. In case studies of elementary students' responses to classroom texts, particularly highly structured kits and leveled texts, there is compelling evidence that students define themselves as readers in relation to these materials. For example, McCarthey found that students in color-coded programs often aligned their view of their reading identity with the predetermined categories or colors of the reading series they were using. The danger here is that students will opt for a narrow, testable level of literacy. As we mentioned earlier, in a global, fast-track society, reading at the most mundane, minimal level simply is not good enough. From an identity construction and critical literacy standpoint, classroom discussions should span both meanings that are specific to the text as well as meanings that go to the heart of critical literacy. Thus, questions of who has power and voice, how people or characters are positioned, and what gaps and silences exist in the text should be explored.

To summarize this section, the following are key elements of identity construction:

- Social context
- Individual interpretation of where one stands in a social context
- Dynamic construction
- Nonessentialist nature

The most promising element of both textual interaction and identity construction is its dynamic nature, offering the hope of agency, self-realization, and change. By developing an understanding of contemporary views of identity construction, you can modify your curriculum to accommodate the need for critical literacy, thereby creating for your students a discursive space where they can consciously use texts to mediate the world and their senses of self.

Am I "Doing" Critical Literacy?

As with any type of pedagogical practice that is named and studied, much debate exists about what "counts" as critical literacy. This type of debate is actually quite productive. Talking about our practices, the benefits, the drawbacks, including the unexpected, helps to keep critical literacy an appropriately complicated, contextualized, and transformative practice. In other words, critical literacy is not just one type of practice with similar kinds of results. It should look and sound different, based on different contexts, participants, and practices.

(Continued)

(Continued)

How, Then, Can I Know If I Am Engaging in Critical Literacy?

Critical literacy, as a label, can often be ascribed to literacy practices that, while valuable, don't engage students in critical stances. For example, asking students to compare two different versions of Cinderella fairy tales, although a higher-order thinking activity, does not include a critical perspective (Knobel & Healy, 1998). For that, questions about representation, benefit, and effects must come into the conversation. While static definitions are not desirable, there are some characteristics that we can point to that mark most critical literacy practices, including, but not limited to, combinations of the following:

- Approaching *all* texts as representational, including some aspects while leaving others out
- Situating a text within particular social, cultural, political, and historical contexts
- Determining what "work" (results, consequences, effects) the text does with certain kinds of readers
- Juxtaposing different texts for differing representations and comparing what work each text is doing
- Engaging in contested and rigorous discussions about a text's representations
- Finding, creating, and promoting alternative textual representations

For example, if you engage students in the development of a community video or podcast documentary,

- To what extent does this form of representation question social practices (e.g., around issues of children's health and welfare, gangs, youth violence, youth opportunities)?
- How do these issues position youth as all the same, different, complex, or stereotypical?

Each of these bulleted items offers some of the ingredients of critical literacy, but as we will see in subsequent chapters, there is much more to this process.

DISCUSSION QUESTIONS

In order to truly grasp the ideas in this chapter, it may be helpful to begin applying some of these notions of dynamic texts and identity formation to your own "reading" of various forms of texts you encounter. For example, as you watch television, explore the Internet, or read magazines you enjoy, ask

- How are various advertisements positioning you as a reader?
- Is the ad gender-specific or gender-biased in nature?
- How are various ethnic groups represented (or not represented)?
- What would change the nature of these ads if they were to be rewritten?

Discuss these findings with other teachers engaged in exploring and implementing critical literacy practices in their classrooms. In addition to texts you locate in your day-to-day environment, also look at contemporary young adult literature, particularly multicultural literature.

- How are characters constructed in terms of representations that essentialize or stereotype gender, race, and socioeconomic dimensions?
- How is the novel constructed to portray particular elements of characters and events, while leaving out others (i.e., gaps and silences)?
- Who has agency and power in the novel?
- Who lacks agency and power?

In summary, applying critical literacy practices to your own reading and moving these practices into your teaching will enable them to become familiar and offer a powerful antidote to lower-level questions.

KEY TERMS FROM THIS CHAPTER

Agency refers to students feeling like they have a voice in a classroom and their opinions and views are valued.

Attention economy is the use of print and digital texts to capture consumers' attention in order to sell products.

Content area literacy is teachers' efforts to guide students' understanding and critique of all forms of texts (print and digital) in subject areas like English, science, social studies, mathematics, art, music, and physical education.

Deconstruction is the analytical process of examining any form of text as non-neutral in terms of race, class, and gender issues, biases, hidden agendas, philosophical underpinnings, and other elements of power in discourse.

Digitally mediated texts are texts in hyperspace, on the Internet, on iPods, and on other nonlinear presentation modes that are typically more fluid than traditional static print.

Essentialist label is a narrow, often stereotypical view of a person reduced to a single term like *skater* that purports to identify and describe identity.

Identity formation: Identity is more than some unified concept, because people have multiple identities in varying social contexts, thus challenging older, narrow definitions of identity.

Metacognitive awareness means literally thinking about thinking and being aware of how digital texts function in the information age.

Metalanguage is critical conversations with students about language in terms of what work texts accomplish through word choice, structure, and underlying elements that go beyond the content of the material.

Positionalities means looking closely at how a text "positions" a reader in terms of race, class, gender, perspective taking, and insider versus outsider perspectives (see the work on positioning theory [e.g., Harre, Lagenhove, & Berman, 1999]).

Socially situated literacy practice: All literacy events, including reading and discussing various forms of texts, are ultimately layered with power dimensions in a classroom so that some students have a presence in discussions while others are silenced due to varying social status, race, class, and gender perceptions and biases. Like a text, no social situation is neutral.

Texts are now broadly defined as cultural tools that include a host of print and digitized forms serving a multitude of purposes (e.g., instant messaging, text messaging, using a smartphone, viewing streaming video, listening to books).

Text genres are identifiable patterns of texts, including narration and expository text patterns (e.g., compare/contrast, problem-solution, chronological listing, pro-con)

In the section that follows, we list key resource texts and Web sites that should be helpful as you undertake incorporating critical literacy in your classroom.

RECOMMENDED FURTHER READING

Dynamic Texts

Goodman, S. (2003). *Teaching youth media: A critical guide to literacy, video production, and social change.* New York: Teachers College Press.

Kist, W. (2005). *New literacies in action: Teaching and learning in multiple media.* New York: Teachers College Press.

Lankshear, C., & Knobel, M. (2002). Do we have your attention? New literacies, digital technologies, and the education of adolescents. In D. E. Alvermann (Ed.), *Adolescents and literacies in a digital world* (pp. 19–39). New York: Peter Lang.

Lynn, S. (2001). *Texts and contexts: Writing about literature with critical theory* (3rd ed.). New York: Longman.

McNabb, M. L. (2006). *Literacy learning in networked classrooms: Using the Internet with middle-level students*. Newark, DE: International Reading Association.

Identity and Culture

Cherland, M., & Harper, H. (2007). *Advocacy research in literacy education: Seeking higher ground*. Mahwah, NJ: Lawrence Erlbaum.

Hagood, M. C. (2002). Critical literacy for whom? *Reading Research and Instruction, 41,* 247–266.

Hagood, M. C., Stevens, L. P., & Reinking, D. (2002). What do THEY have to teach US? Talking 'cross generations. In D. Alvermann (Ed.), *Adolescents and literacies in a digital world*. New York: Peter Lang.

Resources: Podcasts and Wikipedia

Apple iTunes-Podcasts (www.apple.com/podcasting/)

Wikipedia: A constantly evolving digital encyclopedia that is free and based on the Hawaiian word *wiki wiki* for quick (en.wikipedia.org/wiki/Podcasting)

NOTES

1. IMing: Instant messaging. An online chat feature that allows users to hold a written conversation by relaying rapid messages to each other.

2. A fictitious magazine.

REFERENCES

Alvermann, D. E., Moon, J. S., & Hagood, M. C. (1999). *Popular culture in the classroom: Teaching and researching critical media literacy*. Newark, DE: International Reading Association.

Bean, T. W., & Moni, K. (2003). Developing students' critical literacy: Exploring identity construction in young adult fiction. *Journal of Adolescent & Adult Literacy, 46,* 638–648.

Broughton, M. A., & Fairbanks, C. A. (2002). Stances and dances: The negotiation of subjectivities in a reading/language arts classroom. *Language Arts, 79,* 288–296.

Cherland, M., & Harper, H. (2007). *Advocacy research in literacy education: Seeking higher ground*. Mahwah, NJ: Lawrence Erlbaum.

Flake, S. (2001). *Money hungry*. New York: Hyperion.

Gee, J. P. (1996). *Social linguistics and literacies: Ideology in discourses* (2nd ed.). Bristol, PA: Taylor & Francis.

Goodman, S. (2003). *Teaching youth media: A critical guide to literacy, video production, and social change*. New York: Teachers College Press.

Hagood, M. C. (2002). Critical literacy for whom? *Reading Research and Instruction, 41*, 247–266.

Hagood, M. C., Stevens, L. P., & Reinking, D. (2002). What do THEY have to teach US? Talking 'cross generations. In D. Alvermann (Ed.), Adolescents and literacies in a digital world. New York: Peter Lang.

Harper, H. J., & Bean, T. W. (2006). Fallen angels: Finding adolescents and adolescent literacies in a renewed project of democratic citizenship. In D. E. Alvermann, K. A. Hinchman, D. W. Moore, S. F. Phelps, & D. R. Waff (Eds.), *Reconceptualizing the literacies in adolescents' lives* (2nd ed., pp. 147–160). Mahwah, NJ: Lawrence Erlbaum.

Harre, R., Lagenhove, L. V., & Berman, L. (1999). *Positioning theory: Moral contexts of intentional action*. Oxford, UK: Blackwell.

Kist, W. (2005). *New literacies in action: Teaching and learning in multiple media*. New York: Teachers College Press.

Knobel, M., & Healy, A. (Eds.). (1998). *Critical literacies in the primary classroom*. Rozelle, New South Wales, Australia: Primary English Teaching Association.

Langhorne, R. (2001). *The coming of globalization: Its evolution and contemporary consequences*. London: Palgrave.

Lankshear, C., & Knobel, M. (2002). Do we have your attention? New literacies, digital technologies and the education of adolescents. In D. Alvermann (Ed.), *Adolescents and literacies in a digital world*. New York: Peter Lang.

Lewis, C. (2001). *Literacy practices as social acts: Power, status, and cultural norms in the classroom*. Mahwah, NJ: Lawrence Erlbaum.

Luke, A., & Elkins, J. (1998). Adolescent literacy for New Times. *Journal of Adolescent & Adult Literacy, 48*, 525–530.

Lynn, S. (2001). *Texts and contexts: Writing about literature with critical theory* (3rd ed.). New York: Longman.

McCarthey, S. J. (2002). *Student identities and literacy learning*. Newark, DE: International Reading Association.

McCarthey, S. J., & Moje, E. B. (2002). Identity matters. *Reading Research Quarterly, 37*, 228–238.

McNabb, M. L. (2006). *Literacy learning in networked classrooms: Using the Internet with middle-level students*. Newark, DE: International Reading Association.

Moje, E. B., Dillon, D. R., & O'Brien, D. (2000). Reexamining roles of learners, text, and context in secondary literacy. *Journal of Educational Research, 93*, 165–180.

Moje, E. B., & Van Helden, C. (2004). Doing popular culture: Troubling discourses about youth. In J. A. Vadeboncoeur & L. P. Stevens (Eds.), *Reconstructing "the adolescent": Sign, symbol and body*. New York: Peter Lang.

Naidoo, B. (2000). *The other side of truth*. New York: HarperCollins.

Readence, J. E., Bean, T. W., & Baldwin, R. S. (2004). *Content area literacy: An integrated approach* (8th ed.). Dubuque, IA: Kendall/Hunt.

Stevens, L. P. (2001). *South Park* and society: Curricular implications of popular culture in the classroom. *Journal of Adolescent & Adult Literacy, 44,* 548–555.

Stevens, L. P., & Bean, T. W. (2003). Adolescent literacy. In L. Gambrell, L. Morrow, & M. Pressley (Eds.), *Best practices in literacy instruction* (pp. 187–200). New York: Guilford.

CHAPTER 3

Critical Literacy and Teacher Education

In this chapter we look at the impact of recent legislation on teacher identity and explore what futurists and risk analysis experts say about critical literacy. We consider how teacher education might take up a critical perspective to counterbalance forces that may limit students' literacy development within a fluid, fast-moving world of electronic texts. In addition, we provide examples of how both teachers and students use critical literacy, along with a strategy called Resident Critic. We discuss and offer readings on critical media literacy. Finally, we give some attention to the U.S. policy context and propose countermoves based on critical literacy and critical pedagogy. We introduce some of these issues with the following school-based scenario.

School has ended at Ruby Washington Elementary, and a diverse population of young students, many speaking English as a second language, wait for their bus rides home. In the faculty lounge, a small group of teachers are talking about a new scripted reading program their school is thinking about adopting. These teachers are enrolled in a graduate critical literacy course taught on-site in the late afternoon at Ruby Washington, and they are cognizant of many of the concepts covered in the previous chapters in this book. We can listen in briefly on their conversation and get a glimpse of the impact of the course on their professional identities and the need for a critical perspective in various curricular decisions, including text and reading program adoptions. Indeed, as we argue in this chapter, both teachers and their students need to acquire skills in critical literacy that guide judgments concerning curriculum and related policy documents.

Carmen: Well, I know the brochures and ads for this reading program look good, especially for children struggling with the early stages of literacy acquisition. It is comprehensive and covers Grades 1 through 6 with a blend of phonics and comprehension strategies introduced through direct instruction. But as I searched the library and Internet for evaluation reports, this is what I learned. After the early grades, the effects of this program don't last. In fact, by fifth grade, in the large-scale evaluation study I read, nearly 90% of the students served were below grade level as measured by a standardized reading test. In fact, they were over 2.5 years behind their grade level expectancy despite this intervention program in the early grades. What I am saying is, I think we should be cautious and look at various programs or design a curriculum that best serves our students, many of whom speak English as a second language.

Phil: I agree with Carmen and applaud her digging into some of the research that challenges simplistic ads making wild promises. Our kids are too important to just leap into a mandated reading program that takes us out of the loop because it's too scripted. I've heard the term *teacher-proof* used to describe these programs, which completely denies all our years of experience and craft knowledge about our teaching and our kids. Personally, I like a more balanced program of instruction like the Four Blocks (Cunningham & Cunningham, 2002), where children spend 30 to 40 minutes in guided reading, 30 to 40 minutes in self-selected reading, 30 to 40 minutes in writing, and 30 to 40 minutes working with words. That way, the phonics and other decoding drills are applied to real reading tasks, not isolated and abstract.

Matt: Yes. The thing I like about a more balanced program is that there is a transfer to the reading kids have to do. And we can supplement our instruction with children's literature, a variety of decoding exercises, and a host of other material we create, including the stories and little books that our kids produce. I don't want to be locked into a scripted program for our whole reading curriculum, but I might want to borrow some elements from those materials. I really like the notion of being eclectic with a strong instructional rationale for doing so.

Julia: If that's the way we feel, why don't we continue to gather evidence for using a more balanced curriculum like the Four Blocks and also gather research that challenges the notion of adopting a scripted program as the end-all and be-all of our reading curriculum? We can then present our argument to the principal and do the right thing for the kids we're working with. I'd feel a whole lot better about having our professional insights considered in this process, and this approach is in line with the application of critical literacy to policy decision making that we're learning about in this course.

Under the current climate of distrust of public education, teachers are struggling to justify curriculum decisions that will best prepare a thoughtful, critically astute citizenry. Their identities as professionals may flourish within the small world of a graduate class like the one at Ruby Washington, but outside this domain, they often feel their voices are not heard. This lack of agency has its origins in preservice education and extends into inservice experiences where federal and state mandates often limit teacher autonomy.

TEACHER IDENTITY

One of the dominant features of schools during recent years is the degree to which they are expected to replicate and produce conventional, mainstream social meanings, practices, and **subject positions** (Edmondson, 2004; Foucault, 1972; Giroux, 2001; Lesko, 2001; Shannon & Edmondson, 2005). However, schools are not neutral terrain, and in reproducing a mainstream vision of **scientifically based literacy**, the liberating and change functions of schools are placed on the back burner. For example, in many schools in the United States and elsewhere, scripted lessons and behavior management routines diminish the role of the teacher as decision maker and professional educator. Giroux (2001) argues that "knowledge functions as a reproductive force that partially serves to locate subjects within the specified boundaries of class, gender, and race" (p. 224). Skill drills and technical mastery of literacy processes strip away its more powerful social and political power (Giroux, 2001).

In this climate, schools have been reduced to centering instruction on standardized curriculum and high-stakes assessments with the goal of producing technically trained workers for the marketplace (Giroux, 2001). Is this approach working? Analyses of 18 states where high-stakes testing has been in operation for a number of years show the deleterious impact of this movement (Amrein & Berliner, 2003). Significant increases in the high school dropout rate and an increase in students seeking credit recovery programs and general education diplomas outside the confines of the school walls are the result of the current preoccupation with success as measured by high-stakes assessments. Lost in this movement are the caring and social justice interests that engage teachers in a field with relatively low pay and low status. The real high-risk issues are sublimated and reduced to a preoccupation with test scores. Giroux (2001) notes:

> Issues regarding schooling and social justice, persistent poverty, inadequate health care, racial apartheid in the inner cities, and the growing inequalities between the rich and the poor have been either removed from the inventory of public discourse and public policy or factored into talk show spectacles that highlight private woes bearing little relationship either to public life or to potential remedies that demand collective action. (p. xxii)

Teacher identity construction occurs early on in preservice experiences in literacy where language is often stripped of its cultural and political potential. Rather, skills lists, canned commercial programs, and phonics rules predominate to the exclusion of critical literacy and a critique of the institutions of power that disempower teachers' growth as thoughtful, moral, decisive professionals. Bean and Harper (2004) argue that preservice teachers are in a kind of limbo, caught between the worlds of student and teacher. In essence, preservice teachers must negotiate the murky terrain of multiple, and sometimes conflicting, expectations, much like adolescents grappling with identity issues. University supervisors, cooperating teachers, students, and parents all figure into the perceptions that preservice teachers construct as they think about their identities as teachers. In this push-pull arena, preservice teachers may find it difficult to take up a critical literacy stance in their own work, let alone in the often prescriptive curriculum offered in schools.

Inservice teachers find themselves operating not collectively in their first years but often left to their own devices to survive. Britzman (2003) challenged the myth of the teacher as a rugged individual by pointing to the need for collective action and critique of the forces that constrain change in classrooms and teacher preparation. In addition, efforts to cast teachers as "reflective practitioners" (e.g., Bean & Stevens, 2002; Fendler, 2003; Roskos, Vukelich, & Risko, 2001) often overlook the various forms of agency and voice teachers enact amid federal and state mandates surrounding curriculum and assessment policy decisions. Being a reflective practitioner implies the ability to make substantive changes in practice based on reflection. When teachers are able to engage in cooperative critique of the research on lockstep canned programs of instruction in literacy aimed at leveling learners into simplistic categories, it crystallizes their identities as professional educators (McCarthey, 2002).

In contrast, new teacher induction tends to perpetuate a more passive role (Britzman, 2003). In an ongoing 5-year study conducted by Harvard University of 50 new Massachusetts teachers, new teachers were introduced to district policy but little else (Johnson & Kardos, 2002). These teachers reported feeling marginalized and isolated from the sort of collegial, collective support they felt they needed to launch their classroom careers. Rather, classrooms should be sites of ongoing inquiry where classroom practice is examined with an eye toward power relations and policy implications that cut across institutional, social, and global lines (Britzman, 2003; Fairclough, 1989). If we are truly interested in preparing teachers and students to function as involved citizens in the 21st century, then the practice of collective, critical democracy should be evident in schools (Harper & Bean, 2006).

Indeed, this is the sort of discussion the Ruby Washington teachers were having in the opening scenario when they undertook a critique of a proposed program of instruction for adoption at their school. Although education has been called "a profession historically charged with fostering assimilation" (Florio-Ruane, 2001, p. 29), these teachers found ways to critique curriculum through a critical literacy lens. Although engaging in a critique of curriculum adoption proposals with colleagues entails risk, we believe it is absolutely crucial to maintaining a strong and honest pedagogical identity. There are a number of reasons why we feel that critical literacy is more important than ever as a vehicle for maintaining a questioning stance in relation to teaching and policies aimed at reducing knowledge to "idiosyncratic technique" (Hiebert, Gallimore, & Stigler., 2002, p. 7). In a fast-moving global society, simplistic solutions to serious problems of risk are not enough.

RISK, THE FUTURE, AND CRITICAL LITERACY

It used to be enough to rely on scientific experts to manage societal risk in terms of charting an acceptable level of safety in nuclear waste management, global warming, mapping the human genome, cloning, and a host of other real threats to our welfare (Dartnell, 2006; O'Gorman, 2006; Strydom, 2002). In postmodern times, risk is now viewed as a societal concern that should not be left only to engineers and scientists. Vested interests in science and technology want the public to accept risks and often present carefully sanitized versions of what might happen if something goes awry. Contemporary problems related to nuclear waste storage, space travel, energy use and depletion, global warming, and other threats to the biosphere come to mind.

In contrast, there is a growing recognition that human beings create conditions of risk, rendering risk a social construction open to critique and dialogic intervention. Megahazards related to chemical, genetic, and nuclear waste illustrate the postmodern, global impact of risk. There can no longer be a separation of the technical and sociopsychological impacts (Strydom, 2002). In this sphere, experts should be demythologized and open to the critique of an informed citizenry. "Science, technology, industry, capitalism, and the state set processes in train that, despite their operation over peoples' heads and behind their backs, are themselves constituted and guided by cultural models" (Strydom, 2002, p. 88). In essence, developing an informed, democratic citizenry engaged in understanding and influencing policies requires a solid grounding in critical literacy practices (Harper & Bean, 2006). Of course, in literacy, various policy mandates aim to reduce risk by placing curriculum in the hands of technocratic canned instructional schemes that deny teacher agency. While other areas, including ecology and the environment, are open to debate and input in the democratic process, it is truly ironic that curriculum design has taken many steps backward into a modernistic morass. We agree with Strydom (2002), a risk analyst, who argues:

> Through conflict, society is compelled to become aware of and reflect upon the process of development in which it is engaged, what impacts and unilateral consequences follow from it, what knowledge is used, how it is used and for what purposes, but also what knowledge is not used, what is dogmatically clung to, what is exaggerated, what is underplayed, what mistakes are made, what is omitted, as well as the sheer ignorance involved. (p. 60)

Since the 17th century, with a shift from organic nature and craftsmanship to mechanical nature and engineered production, we have relied on experts who often treat society as a boundless laboratory (Strydom, 2002). Without a citizenry taught the theories and methods of critique, we are in danger of eliminating the sort of questioning discourse that defines the democratic process. When teachers like those at Ruby Washington problematize the impact of commercial reading program mandates on their teaching lives, they are helping manage a potentially high risk to society. Indeed, in the new globally connected, Internet-driven public sphere, an informed critical citizenry needs to be able to negotiate a "fluid social space of competing and conflicting communicative structures in which collective agents struggle over the definition of issues and the making and implementation of decisions" (Strydom, 2002, p. 107). For example, public, Internet-based forums where bloggers write and share their views on various topics across geopolitical and global boundaries typify newer cyberspace forms of activism (Dartnell, 2006; Friedman, 2005; O'Gorman, 2006). It seems highly doubtful that children schooled in the "scientifically based" research skills that underpin our current basic literacy curriculum will be prepared for this postmodern world. That is indeed a very high risk.

Rather, we believe that the processes of critique inherent in critical literacy expose and deconstruct taken-for-granted assumptions behind any discourse. It is that critical disposition that must be part of a reader's repertoire in a world in which nature and society are intertwined in ways that create both high risks and great opportunities. Futurists see much of this work occurring in teams, placing a high premium on collaboration and community discourse (Cooper & Layard, 2002). Much of our current mandated curriculum emphasizes individual competition to meet literacy standards that fail to include an alignment with the needs of society and the marketplace futurists have charted. However, various position statements and standards documents do emphasize elements of critical literacy, and these documents can be used to support policies that infuse critical literacy in the classroom. For example, the most recent edition of the *National Science Education Standards* (National Research Council, 2002) takes a sociological turn, specifically mentioning the need for students in Grades 5–8 to understand the risks and benefits of science and technology in society. Thus, policy-setting documents, like this one and others specific to literacy (e.g., the Adolescent Position Statement advanced by the International Reading Association), support teachers' efforts to engage students in a critical analysis of content across curricular areas. At the close of this chapter, we offer a selected listing of position statements and standards documents advanced by various professional organizations that should be helpful in developing and defending the infusion of critical literacy in classrooms. In addition to these documents, there are some very pragmatic reasons why critical literacy is so important in our curriculum.

Multinational governing bodies that have shifted away from vertical, hierarchical decision making call for highly educated, globally aware citizens (Besley, 2002; Friedman, 2005). Supranational events and phenomena, including global warming, tsunamis, financial crises, avian flu, and ideological conflicts, require people who can question and probe decisions rather than relying on experts to do this alone, and lately with frequently negative consequences. Having both a working knowledge of critical literacy and the tools to implement this knowledge are important. In the next section we explore some potentially useful tools for turning discourse inside out with an eye toward transforming teaching practices.

DISRUPTING EDUCATION DISCOURSES WITH CRITICAL LITERACY

Critical literacy requires a different pathway than the dominant, decontextualized approach to teacher education many preservice and inservice teachers experience. In the existing political climate, there is an obvious effort to silence student and teacher voices with prescribed, precanned curriculum packages. Yet there are programs around the country that do introduce teachers to critical literacy practices. For example, Jacqueline Edmondson, a professor at Pennsylvania State University, infuses her classes with theories and direct experiences that treat teachers as inquirers. We can listen in on excerpts from an interview with Jacqueline conducted by Lisa (personal communication, February 12, 2003) to get a flavor for the application of critical literacy in a preservice teacher education program.

Lisa: Critical literacy in your teaching at the university—can you tell me how you found opportunities to do that?

Jacqueline: How will you design your language education program, what will you do—I mean, we do key studies on children to understand how children are learning to read and write. We visit schools. I take my classes to a rural school that's north of here in an economically depressed area so we can talk about what are their understandings of poverty—what are the situations for this particular school and what are the children facing. We'll look at textbooks, we'll look at basal programs, we'll get all of those things so they understand what they are. It goes back to that idea—understanding the context. This is the context in American schools today. Now what is it that we do about it?

Lisa: It's helping them understand the question of what do I do at 9 a.m. on Monday morning but understanding it in terms of the context of where they are.

Jacqueline: Sure. Why they're making the decisions that they're making and what they might do differently. They also have to understand policy and political conditions as they apply to language and literacy education.

Lisa: But I also worry about teachers occupying a fairly unempowered place within the system and wondered about your thoughts about that.

Jacqueline: I think one of the things that I hear from teachers coming into my classes more than anything is their feeling of isolation, particularly if they tend to be progressive teachers in a school that is pretty traditional. One of the things about the courses that I designed specifically is so that teachers can sit and talk with one another. They're beginning to realize their private stories are not private issues.

Lisa: The idea of a teacher as a change agent.

Jacqueline: And developing a sort of shared language and a shared understanding of what's going on. And I think too as an educator, it's
always difficult to sort of strike the appropriate balance between
decentering the power in the classroom and allowing the students
that time to talk.

Lisa: But it's a good point you bring up. It's how a teacher educator
can be a model of how a critical perspective can run through pedagogical approaches.

Jacqueline: I try to model what I hope they would do. I think so much of what's
missing from this is the idea that education is human work. You
need social interaction, you need communication, and language is
essential to all of that. The ways schools are structured increasingly
try to remove the human part of teaching. And when we look at the
implementation of scientifically based reading programs, there's
that alienation that's involved with teachers from their work.

Interestingly, Jacqueline touches on issues that go to the heart of teachers'
professional identities. In a review of research on teachers' views of external
political forces that mandate curriculum decisions, the teachers felt that they
were "being drawn away from what they describe as their central task, namely
helping children and adolescents learn" (van den Berg, 2002, p. 598). In our
view, this is exactly the state of decontextualized thinking critical literacy can
counter if it is part of both teacher preparation practice and inservice teacher
practice. Teaching is highly personal and potentially isolating, as Jacqueline
acknowledges in her work aimed at countering teacher isolation. Indeed, "a shift
from a rational-linear perspective on school development and the professional
development of teachers to a cultural-individual perspective is thus required"
(van den Berg, 2002, p. 613). This shift in perspective to one that embraces critical literacy within teacher development requires a conscious move away from
simplistic, functionalist questions about what works (Edmondson, 2002).
Rather, taking a critical stance means recognizing that curriculum design is
never divorced from values and ideological positions. We argue for a wide-angle
lens on any curriculum in literacy that recognizes its historical and political origins. Thus, in considering any curriculum reform or intervention in literacy, we
would suggest asking one or more of the following critical questions:

- Whose interests are being served by this curriculum?
- Who is not represented in this curriculum?
- How will this curriculum serve students as future learners?

- Are students active or passive recipients of this curriculum?
- What are the historical origins of this curriculum?
- What political stances are served or ignored in this curriculum?

By engaging teachers in conversations that probe behind the scenes into these often hidden spaces of curriculum development in literacy enables them to begin to see how critical literacy offers a vehicle for the critique of practice grounded in their classroom experiences (McClaren, 2000). In essence, we are asking readers to explore larger issues that texts attempt to represent, often in abbreviated forms or in de Certeau's (1984) words: "The text is society itself" (p. 167). Issues of race, class, and gender underpin the design of any text and any curriculum reform. Texts exist at the crossroads of culture and identities where boundaries shift and meaning is unstable (Barker & Galasinski, 2001). Rather than taking a unidirectional, simplistic view of literacy, critical literacy in practice seeks multiple perspectives on texts and multiple voices operating from various wide-angle lenses to deconstruct obvious and less obvious meanings. All texts, including traditional textbooks, as well as popular culture comics, trading cards, films, video games, zines, and IMing (instant messaging), have hidden assumptions and subjective values open to critique if we provide space in classrooms for students to raise critical questions like the ones above (Lewis & Fabos, 2005; Rogers, 2002; Xu, Perkins, & Zunich, 2005). For example, any number of software packages in literacy claim to advance students' reading achievement with built-in reading passages and related assessments. For our purposes, here is an ad for a hypothetical, albeit similar to many, computer-based software package.

The Komodo 1000 Reading Program

The Komodo 1000 Reading Program is a comprehensive software package aimed at developing reading skills in phonics, vocabulary development, comprehension, and fluency across multiple grades. This self-paced, self-managing program of drills frees teachers to be facilitators of learning in their classrooms. The program is Internet-based so that it can be updated easily as new software becomes available. The Komodo 1000 Reading Program removes the guesswork from teaching by starting each student with a diagnostic test of phonics, vocabulary, comprehension, and fluency in order to construct the most appropriate intervention drills. In addition, skills are matched to statewide assessments to ensure that student progress matches standards-based learning goals. The Komodo 1000 Reading Program will replace time wasted on poorly structured reading experiences typical of Sustained Silent Reading and self-selected reading and discussion in Book Clubs.

The Komodo 1000 Reading Program requires high-speed Internet accessibility and a computer for each learner to truly take advantage of its capabilities. Visit the Komodo 1000 Reading Program Web site to explore sample lessons at various grade levels. Based on a substantial investment utilizing Hollywood-style video clips and fast-paced drills, the Komodo 1000 Reading Program is a state of the art package.

Cost of a subscription to this site, while substantial and variable depending upon the needs and goals of a school, is within most curriculum budgets if the cost of more typical print-based material is replaced with the Komodo 1000 package. Call 1-800-932-8949 to talk with a sales representative.

In order to deconstruct a text like the Komodo ad, we can employ some of the key critical questions advanced earlier in the chapter. A group of teachers at Ruby Washington Elementary formed a subcommittee to evaluate the promises of the Komodo 1000 program from a critical stance. We can listen in as they converse about the program in the context of the following critical questions.

- Whose interests are being served by this curriculum?
- Who is not represented in this curriculum?
- How will this curriculum serve students as future learners?
- Are students active or passive recipients of this curriculum?
- What are the historical origins of this curriculum?
- What political stances are served or ignored in this curriculum?

Mavis: The brochure makes some fantastic claims, and our students are captivated by the Internet, from what I can see. But is this program supposed to replace reading books for pleasure? When I took a graduate class at the university last summer, we read some research that showed achievement gains for kids who did the most voluntary, recreational reading in literature [e.g., see Sturtevant et al., 2006]. This program seems to replace our Sustained Silent Reading efforts and pretty much leaves us as teacher robots. Don't we know what's best for kids in our own classrooms, and wouldn't we be giving this professional judgment over to some commercial Internet-based outfit?

John: I agree with Mavis but for a different reason. When I looked at the online demo material for the Komodo program, it seemed pretty boring compared to their claims in the ad. It looked to me like old-style drill and practice curriculum based on Skinnerian behavior management notions. Each activity in phonics, vocabulary development, and so on uses enabling activities to learn sounds of graphemes followed by a test. If a student can't pass the test, they are cycled back into more drills. In essence, they can't move forward until they pass a test, and as I played with the program, it became apparent to me that some of our students would simply get stuck in an endless loop and become frustrated. Where is the teacher in all of this?

Pat: Yes. I think John has hit the nail on the head with the theoretical roots of this program. It's based on an outmoded theory of learning that is anything but constructivist in nature. The learner is treated like a robot along with teachers. It does fit a very narrow view of literacy development consistent with our high-stakes tests, and that's probably why the administration wants us to give it a look for possible adoption.

Mavis: Okay, let's go back to our critical questions and see how this program holds up. First, whose interests are being served by this curriculum? Well, it seems to me that, after looking at the demo lessons, the divergent learning styles and cultural diversity in our Ruby Washington students are largely ignored. The program emphasizes not cooperative group learning but individual competition for test score improvement. All of our past efforts to create a strong, small group learning climate in our classrooms would go out the window if this were our only literacy curriculum!

John: And the Hollywood-style video clips look like a Beverly Hills population of students that really doesn't match our African American and Latino/Latina neighborhood and population. In that sense, our students are not really present in this curriculum, and it violates the strong community/school connections we are trying to develop here.

Pat: When we think about how this curriculum will serve our students as future learners, what I noticed is that the program never really provides that transition to independent application of the skills introduced. In that sense, I think it makes kids and teachers dependent upon the program, and that worries me. All the research we've read in our graduate classes emphasizing scaffolding of instruction in literacy followed by a phasing out of guidance and move toward independent learning seems not to be a part of this program.

Mavis: Are students active or passive recipients of this curriculum? I think we've already answered that one, but the program seems to treat our students as passive learners waiting to be saved by the Komodo 1000 site!

Most of my students love the children's literature I read aloud each week, and they do lots of writing from their own funds of knowledge and experiences. They document this work in portfolios, and we regularly converse about their progress and form task groups as they display a need to learn a particular skill, and I'd hate to give up my active teaching around these needs to some canned and distant Internet-based package that sees all learners alike!

John: I want to play devil's advocate for a minute and suggest that maybe we could just adopt a subset of this package that would help our students with decoding if that's what we want.

Mavis: Didn't you read the disclaimer material before the demo? You can't just adopt a small part of the Komodo 1000. You have to subscribe to the whole thing as a school or district and pay the full fee, which isn't cheap. Basically, we would give up our current materials budget, not to mention our eclectic curriculum philosophy that includes elements like critical literacy, in order to purchase this program. Personally, I'm not excited about doing that, and I just see the effort to shift to this reading program as yet another effort to quell our political and professional voices.

Pat: It's just a way to use technology badly to make it look like we are leading-edge and achievement oriented. I can't support buying it for Ruby Washington School.

Mavis: Let's write our report to the principal.

In this scenario, Mavis, John, and Pat used critical literacy to engage in an analysis and critique of a curriculum brochure and related Internet-based material. While there are many good software packages available, the skepticism applied to the Komodo 1000 appears to have been justified. Thus, critical literacy can be an integral part of both our classrooms and daily curriculum decision making at a school level. Critical literacy and the practice of democracy go hand in hand (Harper & Bean, 2006). Looking behind the smoke and mirrors with questions probing whose interests are served by a literacy program opens up a space to make informed decisions about any discourse we and our students encounter. Linda Darling-Hammond (1998) notes that "[e]ducation for democracy requires not only experiences that develop serious thinking, but also access to social understanding developed by actually participating in a democratic community and developing multiple perspectives" (p. 87). One of the more powerful forms of critical literacy that can be incorporated in our teacher education curriculum is **critical media literacy** (Alvermann, Moon, & Hagood, 1999; Luke, 2002). In the next section we offer an approach to engage teachers in the deconstruction of popular television depictions of family life, a major topical focus of numerous sitcoms. The aim of this example is to illustrate ways in which teachers at various grade levels can take up the application and negotiation of critical media literacy.

CRITICAL MEDIA LITERACY AND TEACHER EDUCATION

The pervasiveness of popular culture seeps into even the most remote communities of the world. Satellite television, DVDs, the Internet, digital and print-based ads, and a host of other consumer-oriented images hover around us all the time. The visual elements in contemporary communication are rapidly overtaking textual elements (Kress, 2003; Van Leeuwen, 2005). These multimedia cry out for the sort of deconstruction and critique we have been talking about in this book, but within teacher education programs it is relatively rare to see this element of critical literacy addressed. If it is not included and modeled in preservice and inservice courses, it is unlikely teachers will include this important element of critical literacy in their own classrooms, particularly in an era of narrow assessments. Yet, a recent analysis of state-by-state performance assessments related to No Child Left Behind shows that many of these tests require a high degree of facility with writing (Baldwin, Readence, & Bean, 2004). The more students have opportunities to engage in written responses to key questions about various forms of media, including popular television shows, the better. Critical media literacy can be defined as helping students learn "how the print and non-print texts that are part of everyday life help to construct their knowledge of the world and the various social, economic, and political positions they occupy within it" (Alvermann et al., 1999, p. 119).

We want to offer one caveat before embarking on a demonstration of an approach to critical media literacy that could be used to demonstrate its potential in a teacher education setting. Much of the focus of critical media literacy is on popular media, particularly television that students find relaxing and pleasurable. Thus, the way this critique is undertaken is crucial, because we do not want to be in the position of demeaning something students find engaging and interesting.

Popular culture invites multiple interpretations, opening a space for students to express a variety of viewpoints (Alvermann et al., 1999). Many ways of having students respond critically to media are possible and only limited by one's creativity. Possible response formats include

- Writing a critique based on teacher questions or a guide with follow-up discussion
- Creating a video that mirrors or disrupts media under critique
- Adopting a teacher role as neophyte, with students serving as popular culture experts

As a way of introducing critical media literacy within teacher education classes in literacy, we recommend developing a demonstration lesson. The one we offer here we call Resident Critic. Our example of how to use Resident Critic is based on an interpretive comparison of the elements of family life depicted in two popular television shows, *The Osbournes* and *Malcolm in the Middle*. Both shows offer a view of family life that leans toward a complex mélange of love amid dysfunctionality, at least by some standards. Resident Critic involves students watching the shows with a question guide teachers and students can construct together. In the section that follows, we offer steps for the development of a Resident Critic lesson, along with a brief example. The same process can be applied to a critique of teen magazine content, music, advertisements, and a host of other popular culture media.

RESIDENT CRITIC

The purpose of Resident Critic is to engage students in a thoughtful exploration of how popular culture treats an issue or topic, in this case, the family. In order for student writing and discussion to be provocative and interesting, scaffolding responses to popular culture media is important.

Steps in Resident Critic

1. Create a series of questions or an observation survey provoking a critical stance

2. Ask students to provide written responses to the questions and be ready to defend their responses in a classroom discussion

3. Inform parents about the goals of the lesson and assuage any content concerns

4. Have students carry out their Resident Critic observations using the questions

5. Engage students in a follow-up discussion and debriefing where they can raise additional questions

In the lesson that follows, students in Robert Montoya's senior psychology class watched *The Osbournes* and *Malcolm in the Middle*. Mr. Montoya created a Resident Critic guide to focus their attention on points for comparison and discussion, with particular attention on similarities and differences in how family roles and responsibilities are portrayed in the two shows and in families outside the media realm. Questions developed for the guide were purposely open-ended to afford multiple interpretations and rich discussion.

Resident Critic Guide

The Osbournes and *Malcolm in the Middle*

1. Describe the particular episode you watched for
   A. *The Osbournes*
   B. *Malcolm in the Middle*

2. Describe similarities you observed in terms of how family life is portrayed in both shows.

3. Describe differences you observed in terms of how family life is portrayed in both shows.

4. Would the day-to-day life of your family make an interesting television show people would tune in to watch? Why? Why not?

5. In your view, do contemporary television shows like *The Osbournes* and *Malcolm in the Middle* show family life in a realistic way?

6. How are males and females portrayed in both shows? Do you agree or disagree with how they are portrayed?

7. If you were going to rewrite either of these shows, what would you change?

8. Other observations?

Mr. Montoya's class spent a week collecting their observations by watching both shows and filling out the guide items. They then gathered in small groups for a discussion of each item. The following composite of their discussion centering on Questions 3 through 6 gives a flavor of how Resident Critic works.

Mr. Montoya: In both *The Osbournes* and *Malcolm in the Middle*, there is an
                  implied perfect family, and that's been the center of many older

shows about family life. How do you see some of the differences in these two shows as far as family life is concerned?

Nick: In *The Osbournes*, a full-time camera records their lives constantly, and in a way, there are funny moments, loving moments, and a lot of chaos.

Nanette: Yeah, the house doesn't look perfect like in *Frasier* or other shows. Instead, the dog whizzes on the bed, animals are everywhere, and the kids are pretty sloppy.

Claire: It looks more like my house with younger brothers who are complete slobs, too many dogs, and two cats! But my family doesn't have heavy metal rock stars like Ozzy, so I don't think anyone would find us all that interesting.

Michael: I agree. But half the time I can't understand what Ozzy is saying, and he walks all stooped over—he's pretty old for a rock star.

Mr. Montoya: What about *Malcolm in the Middle*?

John: It moves a lot faster with constant subtexts and action all the time. I love that show. Compared to *The Osbournes*, it's produced in a very slick way, and Malcolm always talks right to the audience. I don't think there's any comparison—*Malcolm* is better.

Michael: But both shows paint a picture of family life as dysfunctional but loving, so I don't think one is necessarily better than the other. People are used to watching real TV now just as much as fictional TV shows. I like both of them.

Mr. Montoya: Both are based on white families, and they play with the perfect family image portrayed in the older 1950s and '60s shows about family life. We'll take a look at clips from some of those too, and reruns are still on cable from the older shows. What about the way males and females are portrayed in these two shows, especially the mom and dad roles?

Iris: Both moms are really strong, but Malcolm's mom loses it more. She's dealing with her geeky husband and three boys, so that's understandable. She's a strong person, and they all listen to her when she's home and go sideways when she's not.

Rick: Nothing goes right in their lives, and they live in a house with a giant hole in the bedroom where birds and other animals just come in. It's really a great spoof on the perfect family, in my opinion. I think it has features of everyone's family, which in most cases are dysfunctional.

Michael: Both families are loving despite a ton of things always going wrong. The main difference I see is that Ozzy has lots of money and Malcolm's family struggles to make ends meet. So, in that way, I think *Malcolm in the Middle* is closer to most of our experiences.

Iris: The older shows like *I Love Lucy* always had moms who were shown as somehow incompetent, or at least they had to appear incompetent to keep the marriage going. That wouldn't be tolerated now. So, both in *Ozzy* and in *Malcolm,* the women are strong and highly competent.

Mr. Montoya: All television sitcoms eventually run their course, and I think this is especially true of real TV sitcoms. After a while, they lose their audiences to other, newer shows with some unusual twist. Nevertheless, both of these shows break some new ground and somehow represent elements of our own lives, or we probably wouldn't watch them. And both deal with representations of white family life, so we also need to consider other contemporary shows and the ways in which diversity plays out in those settings. For now, though, discuss in your small group any rewrites you would make to the two shows and we'll put those on Post-it notes to consider next time.

Resident Critic can be used to consider a variety of pop culture media. By introducing this and other critical literacy elements within teacher education, we can provide a model for classroom practice. Given the dominant role of media in our lives and that of our students, "it is incumbent on teacher education programs to incorporate critical media literacy studies as part of their curriculum" (Alvermann et al., 1999, p. 119).

Curriculum Critique

Using the example critical questions introduced earlier in this chapter, carry out a critical analysis with other teachers in your building of a literacy curricular package, program, or design used in your school site or under consideration for adoption. Based on this analysis, provide a recommendation to your curriculum specialist about the success or difficulty with this program. The following critical questions should guide your analysis:

(Continued)

(Continued)

- Whose interests are being served by this curriculum?
- Who is not represented in this curriculum?
- How will this curriculum serve students as future learners?
- Are students active or passive recipients of this curriculum?
- What are the historical origins of this curriculum?
- What political stances are served or ignored by this curriculum?
- What existing research supports its use?
- What research traditions informed this research? (e.g., quantitative, qualitative, mixed methods)?

By engaging in collaborative and critical curriculum inquiry and critique of current practices in the school and classroom, teachers at both preservice and inservice levels can become more empowered rather than simply lamenting mandated curricular practices that may be detrimental to students. Indeed, recent case studies of outstanding content area teachers indicates that these professional educators operate from a "principled practices" knowledge base gleaned from direct experience in the classroom (Sturtevant et al., 2006). The notion of principled practices suggests variation in how outstanding teachers conduct their classrooms and moves beyond some mythical "best practices" model. We believe that through the thoughtful application of critical literacy, teachers at all levels can take the reins of curricular decision making using critical questions and research findings to support their positions.

DISCUSSION QUESTIONS

Thinking about your own classroom and curriculum:

- What aspects of your curriculum reading materials could be changed, given the ideas about critical literacy advanced in the first three chapters of the book?
- Who controls these decisions?
- How can you influence curriculum decisions related to critical literacy in your school site, keeping the best interests of students in mind?

In summary, in this chapter we introduced an example of teachers at Ruby Washington Elementary collaborating to critique a scripted reading program. Issues impacting teacher identity at both preservice and inservice levels were considered, contrasting passive and active, collective consideration of curriculum adoption. The importance of critical literacy in a risk society was discussed along with an interview profiling a preservice teacher experience that embodies a critical literacy framework.

Key critical questions to ask of any curricular design were introduced, along with a teaching strategy for critical literacy called Resident Critic. An example of how this strategy can be applied to critical media literacy was offered in conjunction with a consideration of key references in this area. Additional examples of critical literacy in action are offered in the coming chapters.

KEY TERMS FROM THIS CHAPTER

Subject positions is a discursively organized way of being in the world and seeing oneself against the backdrop of possible social positions and practices advanced in various forms of texts. This is a complex notion of identity that recognizes multiple identities and views of the self against a normalized, homogenized, externally produced standard (e.g., the ideal achieving student as defined by grade point average success).

Scientifically based literacy is a classical, modernist faith in measurable objectives and test data in conjunction with literacy instructional practices related to behavioral psychology, including scripted lessons, enabling activities, and direct teaching.

Critical media literacy is a predisposition to examine how print and nonprint texts (e.g., film) serve to construct our knowledge of the world and related social, economic, and political positions people occupy. Given the increased visual element in contemporary forms of digitized text, critical media literacy can include a careful grounding in visual media literacy and semiotic design as a basis for critique. Semiotic design involves paying close attention to the sign systems commonly used in print and nonprint texts, including fonts, diagrams, symbols, and other elements (Van Leeuwen, 2005).

RECOMMENDED FURTHER READING

Teacher Education Issues

Bean, T. W., & Harper, H. J. (2004). Teacher education and adolescent identity. In T. Jetton & J. Dole (Eds.), *Adolescent literacy research and practice* (pp. 392–411). New York: Guilford.

Bean, T. W., & Harper, H. J. (2006). Exploring notions of freedom in young adult literature. *Journal of Adolescent & Adult Literacy, 50*(2), 96–104.

Bean, T. W., & Stevens, L. P. (2002). Scaffolding reflection for preservice and inservice teachers. *Reflective Practice, 3*, 205–217.

Britzman, D. (2003). *Practice makes practice: A critical study of learning to teach* (2nd ed.). Albany: State University of New York Press.

Edmondson, J. (2001). Taking a broader look: Reading literacy education. *The Reading Teacher, 54,* 620–629.

Edmondson, J. (2004). *Understanding and applying critical policy study: Reading educators advocating for change.* Newark, DE: International Reading Association.

Florio-Ruane, S. (2001). *Teacher education and the cultural imagination.* Mahwah, NJ: Lawrence Erlbaum.

Harper, H. J., & Bean, T. W. (2006). Fallen angels: Finding adolescents and adolescent literacies in a renewed project of democratic citizenship. In D. E. Alvermann, K. A. Hinchman, D. W. Moore, S. F. Phelps, & D. R. Waff (Eds.), *Reconceptualizing the literacies in adolescents' lives* (2nd ed.). Mahwah, NJ: Lawrence Erlbaum.

Shannon, P., & Edmondson, J. (Eds.). (2005). *Reading education policy.* Newark, DE: International Reading Association.

Strydom, P. (2002). *Risk, environment and society.* Buckingham, UK: Open University Press.

Young, T. A., & Hadaway, N. L. (2006). *Supporting the literacy development of English language learners: Increasing success in all classrooms.* Newark, DE: International Reading Association.

Position Statements and Professional Standards Documents

International Reading Association. (2003). *Standards for reading professionals.* Newark, DE: Author.

International Reading Association & National Middle School Association. (2001). *Supporting young adolescents' literacy learning.* Newark, DE: International Reading Association.

Moore, D. W., Bean, T. W., Birdyshaw, D., & Rycik, J. A. (1999). Adolescent literacy: A position statement. *Journal of Adolescent & Adult Literacy, 43,* 97–112. Also available at www.reading.org/resources/issues/positions_adolescent.html

National Council of Teachers of English. (1996). *Standards for the English language arts.* Newark, DE: International Reading Association.

National Research Council. (2002). *National science education standards.* Washington, DC: National Academy Press.

Critical Media Literacy

Alvermann, D. E., & Hagood, M. C. (2000). Fandom and critical media literacy. *Journal of Adolescent & Adult Literacy, 43,* 436–446.

Alvermann, D. E., Moon, J. S., & Hagood, M. C. (1999). *Popular culture in the classroom: Teaching and researching critical media literacy.* Newark, DE: International Reading Association.

Dartnell, M. (2006). *Insurgency online: Web activism and global conflict*. Toronto, ON, Canada: University of Toronto Press.

Kress, G. (2003). *Literacy in the new media age*. New York: Routledge.

Luke, C. (2002). Re-crafting media and ICT literacies. In D. E. Alvermann (Ed.), *Adolescents and literacies in a digital world* (pp. 132–146). New York: Peter Lang.

O'Brien, D. (2003, March). Juxtaposing traditional and intermedial literacies to redefine the competence of struggling adolescents. *Reading Online*. Retrieved from www.readingonline.org/newliteracies/obrien2

O'Gorman, M. (2006). *E-crit: Digital media, critical theory, and the humanities*. Toronto, ON, Canada: University of Toronto Press.

Stevens, L. P. (2001). *South Park* and society: Instructional and curricular implications of popular culture in the classroom. *Journal of Adolescent & Adult Literacy, 44,* 548–555.

Williams, B. T. (2003). What they see is what we get: Television and middle school writers. *Journal of Adolescent & Adult Literacy, 46,* 546–554.

Xu, S. H., Perkins, R. S., & Zunich, L. O. (2005). *Trading cards to comic strips: Popular culture texts and literacy learning in grades K–8*. Newark, DE: International Reading Association.

REFERENCES

Alvermann, D. E., Moon, J. S., & Hagood, M. C. (1999). *Popular culture in the classroom: Teaching and researching critical media literacy*. Newark, DE: International Reading Association.

Amrein, A. L., & Berliner, D. C. (2003). The effects of high-stakes testing on student motivation and learning. *Educational Leadership, 60,* 32–38.

Baldwin, R. S., Readence, J. E., & Bean, T. W. (2004). *Targeted reading: Improving achievement in middle and secondary grades*. Dubuque, IA: Kendall/Hunt.

Barker, C., & Galasinski, D. (2001). Cultural studies and discourse analysis: A dialogue on language and identity. Thousand Oaks, CA: Sage.

Bean, T. W., & Harper, H. J. (2004). Teacher education and adolescent identity. In T. Jetton & J. Dole (Eds.), *Adolescent literacy research and practice* (pp. 392–411). New York: Guilford.

Bean, T. W., & Stevens, L. P. (2002). Scaffolding reflection for preservice and inservice teachers. *Reflective Practice, 3,* 205–217.

Besley, T. (2002). The architecture of government in the twenty-first century. In R. N. Cooper & R. Layard (Eds.), *What the future holds: Insights from social science* (pp. 209–231). Cambridge: Massachusetts Institute of Technology Press.

Britzman, D. (2003). *Practice makes practice: A critical study of learning to teach* (2nd ed.). Albany: State University of New York Press.

Cooper, R. N., & Layard, R. (Eds.). (2002). *What the future holds: Insights from social science*. Cambridge: MIT Press.

Cunningham, P. M., & Cunningham, J. W. (2002). What we know about how to teach phonics. In A. E. Farstrup & S. J. Samuels (Eds.), *What research has to say about reading instruction* (pp. 87–109). Newark, DE: International Reading Association.

Darling-Hammond, L. (1998). Education for democracy. In W. Ayers & J. L. Miller (Eds.), *A light in dark times: Maxine Greene and the unfinished conversation* (pp. 97–107). New York: Teachers College Press.

Dartnell, M. Y. (2006). *Insurgency online: Web activism and global conflict.* Toronto, ON, Canada: University of Toronto Press.

De Certeau, M. (1984). *The practice of everyday life.* Berkeley: University of California Press.

Edmondson, J. (2002). Asking different questions: Critical analyses and reading research. *Reading Research Quarterly, 37,* 113–119.

Edmondson, J. (2004). Reading policies: Ideologies and strategies for political engagement. *The Reading Teacher, 57,* 418–429.

Fairclough, N. (1989). *Language and power.* New York: Longman.

Fendler, L. (2003). Teacher reflection in a hall of mirrors: Historical influences and political reverberations. *Educational Researcher, 32,* 16–25.

Florio-Ruane, S. (2001). *Teacher education and the cultural imagination.* Mahwah, NJ: Lawrence Erlbaum.

Foucault, M. (1972). *The archaeology of knowledge.* New York: Pantheon.

Friedman, T. L. (2005). *The world is flat.* New York: Farrar, Straus, and Giroux.

Giroux, H. (1996). Towards a postmodern pedagogy. In L. Cahoone (Ed.), *From modernism to postmodernism: An anthology* (pp. 687–697). Oxford, UK: Blackwell.

Giroux, H. A. (2001). *Theory and resistance in education.* London: Bergin & Garvey.

Harper, H. J., & Bean, T. W. (2006). Fallen angels: Finding adolescents and adolescent literacies in a renewed project of democratic citizenship. In D. E. Alvermann, K. A. Hinchman, D. W. Moore, S. F. Phelps, & D. R. Waff (Eds.), *Reconceptualizing the literacies in adolescents' lives* (2nd ed., pp. 147–160). Mahwah, NJ: Lawrence Erlbaum.

Hiebert, J., Gallimore, R., & Stigler, J. W. (2002). A knowledge base for the teaching profession: What would it look like and how can we get one? *Educational Researcher, 31,* 3–15.

Johnson, S. M., & Kardos, S. M. (2002). Keeping new teachers in mind. *Educational Leadership, 59*(6), 12–16.

Kress, G. (2003). *Literacy in the new media age.* New York: Routledge.

Lesko, N. (2001). *Act your age!: A cultural construction of adolescence.* New York: Routledge Falmer.

Lewis, C., & Fabos, B. (2005). Instant messaging, literacies, and social identities. *Reading Research Quarterly, 40*(4), 470–501.

Luke, C. (2002). Re-crafting media and ICT literacies. In D. E. Alvermann (Ed.), *Adolescents and literacies in a digital world* (pp. 132–146). New York: Peter Lang.

McCarthey, S. J. (2002). *Students' identities and literacy learning.* Newark, DE: International Reading Association.

McClaren, P. (2000). *Che Guevara, Paulo Friere, and the pedagogy of revolution.* New York: Rowman & Littlefield.

National Research Council. (2002). *National Science Education Standards.* Washington, DC: National Academy Press.

O'Gorman, M. (2006). *E-crit: Digital media, critical theory, and the humanities.* Toronto, ON, Canada: University of Toronto Press.

Rogers, R. (2002). Between contexts: A critical discourse analysis of family literacy, discursive practices, and literate subjectivities. *Reading Research Quarterly, 37,* 248–277.

Roskos, K., Vukelich, C., & Risko, V. (2001). Reflection and learning to teach reading: A critical review of literacy and general teacher education studies. *Journal of Literacy Research, 33,* 595–635.

Shannon, P., & Edmondson, J. (2005). *Reading education policy.* Newark, DE: International Reading Association.

Strydom, P. (2002). *Risk, environment and society.* Buckingham, UK: Open University Press.

Sturtevant, E. G., Boyd, F. B., Brozo, W. G., Hinchman, K. A., Moore, D. W., & Alvermann, D. E. (2006). *Principled practices for adolescent literacy: A framework for instruction and policy.* Mahwah, NJ: Lawrence Erlbaum.

Van den Berg, R. (2002). Teachers' meanings regarding educational practice. *Review of Educational Research, 72,* 577–625.

Van Leeuwen, T. (2005). *Introducing social semiotics.* London: Routledge.

Xu, S. H., Perkins, R. S., & Zunich, L. O. (2005). *Trading cards to comic strips: Popular culture texts and literacy learning in grades K–8.* Newark, DE: International Reading Association.

CHAPTER 4

Critical Literacy at the Nexus of Praxis

In this chapter we set the stage for exploring what critical literacy can look like in practice. However, we need to approach these descriptions and applications carefully, as we are reluctant to pinpoint too finitely what "counts" as critical literacy, as it defies any single rendering. However, this reluctance is also mediated by the need to tell concrete stories of how critical literacy has been taken up by some skilled learners and teachers. We are careful to resist specific classroom depictions and hold them up as models of critical literacy, as it is only through practice that the social justice basis to critical theory can, in part, be realized. So we begin by first exploring the need to maintain some ambiguity and variation in the praxis of critical literacy and then discussing what are essential features of this praxis. In the three chapters that follow this one, we provide detailed examples of critical literacy in practice. This chapter sets the theoretical stage for reading these classroom applications.

With every educational theory and perspective, the most frequent question posed is, What are practical strategies with this approach? The question is necessary, purposeful, but also potentially dangerous. If taken without the necessary understanding of theory and constant use of reflection, practices are incomplete. In fact, neither theory nor practice can exist on its own and be effective. Theory without practice is decontextualized conjecture, while practice without theory is at best superficial and at worst unwittingly harmful. In short, what is necessary is **praxis**, that blend of theory and practice that mutually interrogate each other. Building from Paulo Freire's work that underscores much of the liberatory nature of critical literacy, the place of praxis is crucial in critical literacy as a means of social justice. In writing about Freire's philosophy of praxis, Ronald Glass (2001) put it this way: "The practice of freedom, as a critical reflexive praxis, must grasp the outward direction, meaning, and consequences of action, and also its inward meaning as realization and articulation of a self" (p. 18). We can look upon critical literacy as just this type of critical reflexive praxis. We grasp the outward direction by actually engaging with texts and representations in critical ways with our students, and we recast the inward meaning by reflecting upon the role, tenor, and consequences of critical literacy in contemporary classrooms.

The term *praxis* is also readily bandied about in educational circles, including preservice and inservice teacher education. However, to actually achieve the kind of praxis that Freire was advocating, a reflexive viewpoint is essential. **Reflexivity**, in this case, can be understood as a constant, cyclical questioning of the theoretical basis, practical implementation, and overall impact of literacy practices. With the prospect of critical literacy, this relationship of praxis is particularly crucial. As we've discussed (see Chapters 1 and 2), critical literacy is as much about an orientation toward texts as particular sets of questions. In this way, critical literacy should be a refractive practice, one in which teachers engage in a questioning fashion about their classroom practices and the critical nature of those activities. By reflecting during stages of planning and implementation, teachers interested in critical literacy would assess if their classroom practices set the stage for critical engagements with text. Looking for opportunities taken to question texts causes a form of praxis occurs. We engage in practices that are informed by theories that undergird critical literacy, but we also reflect upon our practices and use them to better understand and alter those theoretical concepts. There are not, nor should there be, static lists of approaches, sequences, and strategies that qualify as critical literacy across contexts. Rather, critical literacy is "done," in part, by engaging it as praxis, as a combination of both theory and practice, and by keeping it elusive of a static set of practices.

MAINTAINING CRITICAL LITERACY AS A MOVING TARGET

Consider the college textbooks that you read in your teacher education program. Many of them encompass phrases such as "best practices." In fact, as authors and researchers, we have both written about best practices in the field of literacy. However, we suggest that with many areas, and certainly with critical literacy, this type of language and perspective is more self-defeating than helpful. The phrase "best practices" connotes that some specific strategies, approaches, and qualities are necessary and even replicable across contexts. In education and in other fields that work with application of theories to specific settings, a common occurrence is the following sequence: a pedagogical approach is theorized, history and research are provided to support the use of the approach, and then sample lessons and strategies are offered as models for implementing the approach. This same sequence is offered time and time again and leads to a unidirectional flow from theory to practice. Publishing companies, policymakers, and colleagues offer sample or model lessons. Often, publishing companies provide frameworks for teachers, including lesson plans, accompanying materials, assessment of student work, and correlations to state objectives. These offerings are made and taken up readily because of many factors, including the tight time constraints that teachers face as part of their daily work. With the bulk of their days spent in isolation from professional dialogue and with limited time for planning, educators are prime targets for prepackaged materials that overemphasize particular methods over the reflective practice that characterizes the most productive pedagogies for students. Ultimately, many approaches falter, in part due to this unidirectional sequence from ideation to implementation. Without a reflexive stance that questions if the starting purposes and theories are being achieved, if they are still appropriate, and how they might be altered in the future, a flow from theory to practice falls short of becoming praxis.

For critical literacy, the prospect of prepackaged lessons *is* particularly problematic. Critical literacy is, more than anything, about representation and context, asking what work a text is doing in a particular context, with particular readers, and in what ways. How these questions are posed, who takes them up, and what their potential outcome might be is productively elusive of prediction. Taken too literally, explorations of critical literacy in the classroom can quickly escalate into merely getting through a time block with students rather than engaging in serious critique and reflection. In essence, a sociocultural and critical stance on literacy is more about a framework or view of literacy than methods, approaches, or sequences to lessons. We resist providing a set definition of critical literacy and advise others to be wary of approaches that do offer easy definitions and hold up models of best practices. Critical literacy will realize its potential if it remains elusive of a definition, if it, in essence, stays a moving target.

By shifting its shape across contexts and readers, critical literacy then would beg the reflexive questions that interrogate various uptakes and interpretations. Imagine that you and the teacher next door both attend an inservice on critical literacy. As with many professional development approaches, this inservice is an after-school presentation in which critical literacy is defined and then sample lessons and approaches are provided. As you return to your respective class-rooms, you both decided to try adapting and implementing a few of the lessons discussed in the inservice, and you compare notes after these sessions. You might discuss how the students reacted to being asked to engage with texts from a critical perspective, how discussions developed, and if your classroom contexts seemed to be appropriate settings for these types of discussions. This type of exchange and professional dialogue is at the heart of keeping critical literacy elusive of a definition and engaging in praxis. By discussing varying interpretations to critical literacy, you can keep the focus on essential features and not overly technical implementation of too-specific sequences of strategies.

ESSENTIAL FEATURES OF CRITICAL LITERACY

Maintaining critical literacy as a moving target and discussing its varying incarnations across settings also sheds light on those grand features that are found in differing contexts. In the next section, we go further into detail about the necessary components of stance, contexts, tools, and process that have marked successful critical literacy practices. In making critical literacy a hall-mark of our practices as readers, educators, and researchers, we have gathered together a number of salient, essential features that mark this kind of work. Our word choice of *features* is purposeful here, as these characteristics are much larger in nature than strategies, tactics, or activities. Rather, they are large, or grand, qualities of these textual interactions, but they will take shape differently in varying contexts and with diverse participants. With a strategy, such as a think-pair-share activity, we might expect to see the same basic flow of procedure across different classrooms. However, with critical literacy, we have to alert ourselves to creating and reflecting upon features that act as foundations to the set of practices that might count as critical literacy. In fact, they are features of any textual interaction, but we describe the particular ways that they can be engaged to promote the critical questioning of power and texts.

Stance: Texts as Representations

The first component to critical literacy is the necessary feature of a particular epistemic **stance**, or orientation toward texts. For critical literacy to occur, readers must be able to grasp and hold up all texts as representational. While this sounds rather obvious, the implications and ramifications of this attitude toward texts are significant. First, seeing all texts as representation raises two immediate questions: What is included and who has made that decision? These two first questions help to show the biased nature of all texts. By definition, a representation is both an abstraction of its ideas and is partial. Representations leave in some aspects of ideas and leave out others. No representation can fully include and discuss all possible ideas, so choices are made. In first seeing all texts as representational, readers understand that all texts can and should be subject to questions about these choices.

This view is crucial for critical literacy to occur, and it must be a constant feature of textual engagement. To promote this stance with some texts and not others communicates an implicit but powerful message that only some texts are representations. This belies the very nature of critical literacy. Furthermore, invoking this stance in some situations and not others may also prompt students to follow the lead of the teacher in responding to texts. In other words, the readers in the classroom learn to "student," to detect when to respond in critical ways and when not to. This kind of all too familiar pattern in education removes students from a more fully developed and integrated interaction with texts as independent, critical readers, because their attention is partially devoted to detecting when to use critical perspectives. This stance of seeing all texts as representations, then, must be a constant orientation.

Contexts: The Classroom as a Democratic Environment

Another feature of critical literacy, particularly for educational settings, is the context of a **democratic classroom**. By democratic classroom we do not mean the often-invoked example of taking a numerical vote on whether to read this book or that book. Rather, we point to the features of a democratic environment in which participants engage in deep discussions about difficult questions related to power, agency, rights, and harm (Harper & Bean, 2006; Parker, 2003).

For critical literacy to occur, particular questions of representation, power, and ideas are taken up. For example, a key question posed in critical literacy is, What is this text trying to do to me? This question prompts readers to question not only the purpose of the author but also the intended consequences on particular kinds of readers. However, the answers to this type of question defy right/wrong categories, instead invoking plausibility and justification as means to assessing and juxtaposing differing versions. Various interpretations can and should be engendered with these types of questions, and these interpretations can only be shared in a context that values and embodies democratic discourse. This type of discourse involves the engaged tussling over ideas that provides texture and deepens participants' understandings of the text and themselves in relation to it.

Tools: Metalanguage

Perhaps the most technical feature of the practice of critical literacy is the necessary component of metalanguage. Put simply, metalanguage is language about language. In critical literacy, we are particularly concerned with how texts do the work that they try to do. By asking questions about the particular representations and discussing our interpretations, we discuss textual features, including language choices, tone, images, layout, and so on. To engage in these discussions, we need not only an environment that encourages democratic discourse, but we also need the linguistic tools, or vocabulary, to be able to discuss the texts. An easily accessible example *is* found in discussing the kinds of visual images chosen to promote meanings in a high school textbook (see Chapter 1). A more detailed example is a discussion in which students are discussing the possible purposes used by an author who writes in the passive voice. This metalanguage can be, as seen through these examples, micro or macro in nature. That is, the metalanguage can cover broad textual features such as tone, layout, packaging, or it can be far more detailed to the level of syntactical and semantic choices made by the author. Without these linguistic tools, or metalanguage, our abilities to talk about texts themselves are very limited.

Process: Cycles of Deconstruction and Reconstruction

The last feature that we discuss is the cycle of **deconstruction** and **reconstruction** of texts. In engaging critical questions such as who stands to benefit, who is represented here, and who is not represented, we are, in essence, deconstructing texts. We use metalanguage to pick apart the specificities of power, representation, and purpose laden in all texts. Deconstruction of texts is a hallmark not just of critical literacy but of critical theory in general, which pushes readers to scratch beneath the surface. However, a frequent critique of this critical approach is that it leaves skilled readers with figurative pieces of texts strewn about. If all texts are representations, then all texts are subject to deconstruction, and this ability to interrogate texts for their implications of power may, ironically, leave readers feeling nihilistic and at a loss of agency. They may, in other words, feel capable of deconstructing any text and at a loss for finding spaces of empowerment, agency, or efficacy.

To alleviate this potential cul-de-sac of textual practice, moments of reconstruction are necessary to reengage critical readers and to take up further notions of social justice. In reconstruction (see Chapter 7 for a detailed example), readers might recast the text from a different perspective, find alternative texts that privilege different voices, or create their own text. Any of these options are taken up with explicit and democratic discussions of what kinds of representations are more preferred, suitable, and appropriate with the particular sets of values, practices, and purposes. All of these aspects are up for grabs, so to speak, but the reconstruction of texts reengages readers with the choices that they make as readers and also creators of texts. Coming from a critical literacy perspective, they return to texts with the conscious decision about the type of representations that resonate with their worldviews and experiences.

In summary, we have outlined four key features of critical literacy teachers need to consider: (1) stance: texts as representations, (2) contexts: the classroom as a democratic environment, (3) tools: metalanguage, and (4) process: cycles of deconstruction and reconstruction. These four features of critical literacy in practice are by no means an exhaustive and scientifically validated and adjudicated treatise. We would argue that such an endeavor is contrary to the larger epistemic stance that critical literacy promotes. In fact, we hope that you have discussions about these features and their relationship to what you have experienced as readers, students, and teachers. We offer these features and our understandings of them in the hope that you will, as practitioners of critical literacy, engage in your own discussions about these features and in what ways you've seen them enacted and taken up.

Cautions to Engaging in Critical Literacy in the Classroom

- Include recursive cycles of deconstruction and reconstruction. Build agency and empowerment by providing spaces to find and contrast alternative texts.

- Respect students' out-of-school literacy practices and texts. Resist commodifying and "schoolifying" texts and practices that serve other purposes.

- Keep in mind that for many students, critical literacy perspectives and questions have not been part of their experiences in schooling. As with any departure from expected routine, multiple explanations may be necessary.

- Engage critical literacy as a perspective and tone of the classroom. These are not stand-alone activities that can be engaged some days and then not honored on others. Critical literacy is a way of engaging with texts as representational and should be engaged as part of what fluent, competent readers do consistently.

DISCUSSION QUESTIONS

1. Education is known for its successive fads in theories and practices. Discuss what educational fads you have seen come and go and why you think their shelf lives were limited.

2. Often, implementation of theory into practice results in a revision of the original theory or idea. Provide an example of a theory or concept that you implemented in your teaching and how it differed from the originally stated idea.

3. Being a reflexive teacher is discussed in this chapter, as well as in much of teacher education, as a key to successful pedagogy. However, there are many constraints (time, curricular) on engaging in reflective practice. Discuss what constraints you feel as a teacher and how these constraints can be negotiated and mediated.

RECOMMENDED FURTHER READING

Comber, B., & Simpson, A. (Eds.). (2001). *Negotiating critical literacies in classrooms.* Mahwah, NJ: Lawrence Erlbaum.

Davies, D. (1994). *Shards of glass: Children reading and writing beyond gendered identities.* Cresskill, NJ: Hampton Press.

Freire, P. (1970). *Pedagogy of the oppressed.* New York: Herder & Herder.

Gale, T., & Densmore, K. (2000). *Just schooling: Explorations in the cultural politics of teaching.* Buckingham, UK: Open University Press.

Gutmann, A. (1987). *Democratic education.* Princeton, NJ: Princeton University Press.

Gutmann, A., & Thompson, D. (2001). *Why deliberative democracy?* Princeton, NJ: Princeton University Press.

Morgan, W. (1997). *Critical literacy in the classroom: The art of the possible.* London: Routledge.

Muspratt, S., Luke, A., & Freebody, P. (Eds.). (1997). *Constructing critical literacies: Teaching and learning textual practices.* Cresskill, NJ: Hampton Press.

Parker, W. C. (2003). *Teaching democracy: Unity and diversity in public life.* New York: Teachers College Press.

REFERENCES

Glass, R. D. (2001). On Paulo Freire's philosophy of praxis and the foundations of liberation education. *Educational Researcher, 30(2),* 15–25.

Harper, H. J., & Bean, T. W. (2006). Fallen angels: Finding adolescents and adolescent literacy(ies) in a renewed project of democratic citizenship. In D. E. Alvermann, K. A. Hinchman, D. W. Moore, S. F. Phelps, & D. R. Waff (Eds.), *Reconceptualizing the literacies in adolescents' lives* (2nd ed.). Mahwah, NJ: Lawrence Erlbaum.

Parker, W. C. (2003). *Teaching democracy: Unity and diversity in public life.* New York: Teachers College Press.

CHAPTER 5

Praxis Point 1

Popular Culture, Fandom, and Boundaries

In the next three chapters we offer examples of praxis: specific, classroom-based examples of critical literacy, combined with a reflexive interrogation of those practices. With each snapshot, we provide a description of the setting, participants, and activities and then move to reflect upon this usage of critical literacy. In reviewing these examples, we are not as concerned with "did it work?" but a more textured perspective for determining how these instances of practice can help to inform the theory of critical literacy. These chapters also provide detailed examples to explore the limitations, cautions, and drawbacks to using critical literacy in educational spaces. This multidirectional flow between theory and practice helps to achieve the praxis described in Chapter 4. In that sense, we offer these chapters not as models of critical literacy but as contributions to a praxis conversation about how the theory and practice of critical literacy can maintain itself as a substantive, malleable, and permeable set of characteristics.

SNAPSHOT 1: CRITICAL MEDIA LITERACY AND SOCIAL STUDIES

Setting the Context

Craig Weeks was teaching eighth-grade social studies, and Lisa was working at the same school as a literacy specialist. Craig and his classes were reaching the end of the year, and the upcoming unit and chapter focused on U.S. history in the 1960s. Craig had been interested in incorporating inquiry into popular culture, and because the history textbook depicted popular culture trends from the 1960s, he saw this as a perfect way to bring in conversations about popular culture. In working with Craig, Lisa suggested that he also use critical literacy as a way of asking what work the popular culture texts were doing with particular populations. As they planned the unit together, Craig and Lisa maintained a focus on the following critical literacy questions:

1. What popular culture is represented in this text?

2. Who is the intended audience?

3. Who stands to benefit from the use of this text?

4. Who is left out, marginalized, or silenced through this popular culture text?

5. What is the text trying to do *to* its readers?

These questions, in fact, are the quintessential questions of critical literacy: those that seek to situate the text within political, cultural, and economic contexts and also provide the reader with a position to potentially disrupt and/ or resist the text. To model the use of this critical approach to multimediated texts, Lisa and Craig each brought in popular culture texts from their teenage years, which elicited humorous responses from the students and also gave them an opportunity to practice critical literacy perspectives with texts that were not close to them.

In exploring clips from Michael Jackson's dance videos, popular films from the 1980s, and magazine clippings about other celebrities, Lisa and Craig went through a model deconstruction of these texts, demonstrating the importance of plausibility and metalanguage. In modeling plausibility, Lisa and Craig tried to demonstrate that while different readings can exist of a singular text, a reader who makes a claim about one particular ideological stance has to show plausibility. In one instance, they purposefully talked about their differing interpretations *of* a popular culture text, to demonstrate that in a critical and democratic discussion, plausibility takes precedence over uniform interpretation. Rather than quickly arriving at the "right" answer, the goal is to build a more open context for sharing differing viewpoints.

In showing plausibility for their interpretations, Lisa and Craig used metalanguage in discussing the texts. They drew upon specific language to discuss semantic, visual, and representational choices made in the texts. For example, they focused on terms such as *image, tone, music choices,* and *cultural referent points.* They modeled the use of this language to provide students with some of the expected tools that they hoped to see in the students' critical work.

In handing over the assignment to the students, Craig and Lisa asked the students to conduct similar inquiries into contemporary popular culture texts. Students could choose any text they wanted, with restrictions and reminders given about bringing in representations that were appropriate for the classroom context. Students worked in groups to select a popular culture text, discuss the critical literacy questions, and prepare a 5-minute presentation to the class about their findings, conclusions, and perspectives. The following is an excerpt from one group's discussion of the popular TV series *South Park.*

Cody, Justin, and Joshua chose to highlight *South Park* (1997). All three watched the show and reveled in the foul language and discriminatory jokes made by the show's animated main characters. The group members decided that it would prove too difficult to find a clip of the show that was consistent with school district policy, so they opted to create a poster display that showed images of the main characters and included their synopsis of the critical inquiry questions.

Craig and Lisa learned a lot about the students' grasp of the positioning of popular culture. When Cody was presenting his group's work about *South Park,* he adeptly pointed out that several groups stood to be hurt by the show. "This is not intended for Jewish people. Cartman [one of the main characters of the show] always [picks on] Jews and [teases] Kyle because he is Jewish." The boys proved quite adept at providing examples of situations from the show to demonstrate their points without crossing lines of inappropriateness.

Joshua concluded by hypothesizing that "*South Park* is popular with kids because we are always supposed to be so polite, but we still have the same kinds of thoughts and stuff. We just aren't supposed to say them." A small group discussion then ensued in which we talked about political correctness and the backlash we see to this. Here's an excerpt:

Lisa: So, what you guys are saying is that people are sick of being politically correct?

Justin: Yeah, I mean it's not just *South Park.* What about Austin Powers [1997, 1999, 2002]? He's nasty, and everybody loves it.

Lisa: So do *South Park* and the Austin Powers movies appeal to the same audience?

Yolanda: Yes and no. More kids like *South Park,* but it's mostly white people who like both.

Lisa: [To the group who just presented] You guys are nodding your heads; do you agree with that?

Joshua: Yeah, like I went to the second Austin Powers movie last weekend, and I don't remember there being any black people in it [at] all, like they weren't around or something.

During a discussion that followed 2 days' worth of presentations, Craig noted that not all the inquiries achieved the depth that Justin, Joshua, and Cody's did. Overall, he expressed a high level of satisfaction with student involvement and thought. The greatest difficulties in achieving the goals of the unit were presented by those groups who did not have enough time to complete their projects. While using inquiry at the end of the school year helped the teacher and students get through a normally antsy time of year, it also placed some strict time limitations on a unit that had held relevance and inquiry as two key features—features that do not always yield well to external time constraints.

REFLECTION: PRACTICE INFORMING THEORY

At the end of this unit, Craig and I both felt that it was a great success. We felt that the approach's success was due to two key factors: (1) the modeling of critically fueled deconstruction and metalanguage and (2) the student choice of which contemporary texts to bring into the classroom. First, we took the time to make explicit and model what kinds of literacy and textual conversations were expected in this project. We differentiated between critical questions and the kind we more typically ask students to answer in classroom settings. Asking people to engage with critical literacy without providing firsthand interactions with what that might look like could potentially set up learners to have little else to rely on than their past work as students. However, this must be done carefully to avoid providing too narrow *exemplars* that students will deftly mimic without generating original perspectives of their own. Through our experience in this project, the classroom discussions quickly showed whether students were engaged in a democratic discourse about the textual interpretations or if they were merely paying lip service to the teachers' expected textual performance. We felt confident that, due to the dissension and engaged conversation that took place, the students who worked with us in this project truly grappled with these critical questions.

The other key aspect to this project was providing choice and latitude to the young people about the popular culture texts that they wanted to bring in to the classroom to deconstruct. While advertising and popular culture texts have been a common first target of critical literacy, we felt it very important to avoid assuming adultist stances and infringing upon students' fandoms.

As Donna Alvermann and Margaret Hagood (2000) point out in their article about **critical media literacy** and fandom, as contemporary citizens in a media-saturated culture, virtually everyone participates in some form of fandom. While we tend to associate the term *pop culture* with young people, the phrase simply connotes a text that is mass communicated and consumed. Myriad niches of culture fall into this category, including rock, hip hop, genealogical books, knitting, stock car racing, professional sports, and so on. Even recent fads of politically oriented blogs are forms of mass-mediated culture, reaching out to a particular audience in an easily accessible format and using commonly understood reference points, language, and representations to communicate. From this stance, associating popular culture with young people and then critiquing only those perceived forms of popular culture belies the concept of mass-mediated culture and assumes adultist stances toward young people. Done from the complicated and hegemonically tinted relationship between teacher and student and within the institutional space of the classroom, this type of unidirectional flow of critique has several dangers inherent in it, and in the preceding lesson we tried to avoid these pitfalls.

We all interact with particular texts for different reasons, and pleasure is often one of the key purposes for reading, viewing, and listening to texts. An infringement upon this pleasure is an abrogation of understanding the various reasons for interacting with texts and a disregard for the particularly hegemonic relationships that mark teacher/student interactions. The students were allowed complete choice in which popular culture texts they deconstructed and presented to the teachers and their fellow students. In this way, they could set aside texts whose pleasure-driven readings they did not wish to disrupt. While some students chose to do this, we found, through talking with them, that many of them actually chose to bring in texts they supported, engaged with, and purchased for pleasure reasons. They took this opportunity to demonstrate the existing reasons behind their decisions. As in the discussion included in the snapshot, we found that students were more than able to cogently articulate their critical understandings and negotiated engagements with popular culture texts.

This example of critical literacy is fairly common, one that occurs fairly frequently as teachers put this theory into practice. After completing this exercise, though, what can the theory of critical literacy gain from this practice? There are two key lessons to be learned from the critical deconstruction of texts. First, a limitation of this classroom exercise and others like it is the use of deconstruction without reconstruction. While the students were more than able to deconstruct texts and engage in deep discussions about the particular views, agendas, and purposes sitting behind the texts, they did not have the chance to engage in reconstruction. A developing critique of critical theories is that they deconstruct, examine, and critique but often do not engage in reconstructive actions following these analyses. When people begin to appreciate that any text is a representation and can therefore be deconstructed for its particular biases, ideologies, and worldviews, a sense of agency can elude readers. In other words, providing and modeling the terms and tools necessary for critical literacy can equip readers to be agile and nimble deconstructers, but they may then be left with little more than figurative pieces of text surrounding them. If all texts are representational, then all texts can be deconstructed, often to the goals of pinpointing dominant and potentially harmful discourse. While this is a major tenet of critical literacy, it can also lead readers to a feeling of nihilism or hopelessness.

Although Freire argued that the mere process of raising consciousness was, in itself, an act of agency, this is true for some textual practices but not across the board for all readers. To maintain critical literacy as an efficacious and liberatory practice, we suggest that cycles of reconstruction must also occur. These reconstructions can occur in myriad ways, including the re-creation of texts, the location of alternative texts, or the juxtaposition of existing texts. Whatever tactic is employed, the opportunity to reconstruct texts is an important vehicle for readers to consider what representations are most valid to them, for what purposes, and to work toward offering those texts into the conversation.

A second limitation of this exercise and potentially of the field of critical media literacy is found in applying critical questions to media texts only. As we have discussed elsewhere in this volume (see Chapter 1), to move first and/or exclusively to media texts with critical questions flirts with the implicit message that only these texts are in need of such interrogation. This, by default, implies that only these types of texts are representational and biased in nature. As we discussed in Chapter 4, one key feature of critical literacy is a stance, attitude, and epistemology that sees all texts, print or digitally mediated, as representational. If students are primarily asked to engage critical questions with media texts, they may come to understand that other texts have a higher empirical truth basis to them, a perception that runs counter to the foundational concepts of critical literacy.

Students' hobbies or chosen sports often have related magazines that offer pointers, products, and ads (e.g., skateboarding, wrestling, rowing, cars, computers, acting, modeling, to name just a few). Have students bring in one selected magazine that relates to their avocation and, in small groups, engage students in deconstructing and reconstructing ads, advice articles, or other sections of these publications. Consider the following discussion questions or adapt these to better fit your students:

(Continued)

(Continued)

- What popular culture is represented in this text?
- Who is the intended audience?
- Who stands to benefit from the use of this text?
- Who is left out, marginalized, or silenced through this popular culture text?
- What is the text trying to do *to* its readers?

As a writing activity, students can create new versions of the discourse that transform often gendered and biased portrayals of various sports and activities.

DISCUSSION QUESTIONS

1. The suggestion of bringing popular culture texts into the classroom is far from a new idea in education. What experiences have you had with interacting with students' popular culture texts? Have you seen examples where some of these texts have been banned from school? If so, discuss why these reactions may occur and how critical literacy might interact with texts that are seen to be controversial.

2. A key feature of the classroom snapshot in this chapter is the aspect of student choice in deconstructing popular culture texts. One reason for allowing student choice is to respect those textual practices that qualify as pleasure reading or consumption. Share what texts (print, digital, multimediated) are pleasure texts for you and if you would want to approach these texts from a critical stance.

RECOMMENDED FURTHER READING

Alvermann, D. E., Moon, J. S., & Hagood, M. C. (1999). *Popular culture in the classroom: Teaching and researching critical media literacy.* Newark, DE: International Reading Association.

Alvermann, D. E., & Hagood, M. C. (2000). Critical media literacy: Research, theory, and practice in New Times. *Journal of Educational Research, 3,* 193–205.

REFERENCES

Alvermann, D. E., & Hagood, M. (2000). Fandom and critical media literacy. *Journal of Adolescent & Adult Literacy, 43,* 436–446.

Emmerich, T., Brener, R., Lyons, J., McLeod, E., Moore, D., Myers, M., et al. (Producers) and Roach, J. (Director). (2002). *Austin Powers: Goldmember* [Motion picture]. United States: New Line Cinema.

Langley, D., De Luca, M., Stoff, E., Lyons, J., McLeod, E., Myers, M., et al. (Producers) & Roach, J. (Director). (1999). *Austin Powers: The Spy Who Shagged Me* [Motion picture]. United States: New Line Cinema.

McLeod, E., Moore, D., Myers, M., Polstein, C., Todd, J., & Todd, S. (Producers) & Roach, J. (Director). (1997). *Austin Powers, International Man of Mystery* [Motion picture]. United States: New Line Cinema.

Parker, T., & Stone, M. (Creators). (1997). *South Park* [Television series]. New York: Comedy Central.

CHAPTER 6

Praxis Point 2

Critical Numeracy
Across the Curriculum

In the praxis example explored in Chapter 5, several key issues arose from the social studies-based interaction with popular culture texts. These issues have implications both for the practice and theorization of critical literacy. However, as with any blend of theory and practice, differing issues alight with alternate implementations, according to both the particular goals and practices as well as the context and participants. In this next example of a classroom-based approach to critical literacy, we explore issues of curricular applications and metalanguage.

**SNAPSHOT 2: CRITICAL
LITERACY ACROSS THE CURRICULUM**

Setting the Context

At the time of their work together, Diana Hanson taught second grade and was taking a graduate course in content area literacy, taught by Lisa. Although most of the other students in the class were secondary teachers, Diana was working on her master's degree in reading and had a keen interest in revitalizing her literacy pedagogical practices. She had been teaching for several years and had grown both comfortable and complacent with her tried-and-true approaches of reader response interactions in workshop contexts.

As Diana learned more about critical literacy, she became anxious to explore this in her classroom, particularly because the graduate course context explored the myth that critical literacy is more suited to older readers than younger readers. Diana decided to focus in on one curricular area and bring in critical literacy with digital literacy practices. She began working with her second-grade students to increase their interactions with online texts related to science. As Diana worked to increase her students' online interactions with texts both in class and outside of school, she found many teachable moments arise about textual interactions. Several of these teachable moments had to do with gaining acumen with various pragmatic skills in digital literacy, including searching for information and determining criteria for a valid source of information. As Diana and her students moved through these classroom interactions, she took time to debrief the minilessons and learning moments that occurred. During these debriefing times, Diana would explain particular strategies and how they differed from past strategies that the students had explored, and the students would also volunteer observations and insights that they had made about their own literacy practices.

In one such discussion with them, she found that they, like most anyone who uses the Internet regularly, were annoyed by the frequent pop-up advertisements that vied for their attention and distracted them from their original purposes for reading. At this point Diana decided to invite Lisa into her classroom to help map out a more developed approach to exploring the use of the single, but frequently used, word *free* in online pop-up advertisements.

In talking further about these advertisements with the students, Lisa and the students agreed that many of the advertisements used the word *free* to entice readers to click on the advertisement and explore the product or service being advertised. Diana and Lisa decided to tap into the students' annoyance with these advertisements to engage in critical explorations of these texts and, in particular, their uses of the word *free*.

Diana and Lisa framed the critical literacy exercise as an investigation of what counted as "free," according to these advertisements. In essence, the goal was to capture differing representations of "free." The students worked in small groups, and each group tackled thematic bundles of these pop-up advertisements; that is, they focused on collective areas of advertisements and their uses of the word. For example, one group explored the free enticements used by video rental services while another group collected examples of free services offered by online warehouses. Each group tracked the advertisements' uses of the word *free*, the actual costs involved in receiving the product or service, and how particular commercial interests were linked together through the digitized texts. As each small group worked, they were charged with keeping track of the terms and words they used to search, plotting the findings of their search and analysis, and representing their findings and conclusions to the rest of the class.

Patrick, Rachael, and Denise investigated pop-up advertisements that offered diet and weight loss products and services. They came across this topic after they became frustrated by searching for information on calorie burning for a science investigation into various forms of energy use. The more they searched, the more they found themselves being interrupted and potentially lured to sites that had very little scientific basis to them but did speak about calorie burning and weight loss. As they decided upon this topic for their group's exploration, they found no shortage of such pop-up advertisements and Web sites. They changed their keyword searches to include *calorie, energy, weight loss,* and *diet.* To plot their findings of the use of the word *free* in the resulting pop-up advertisements, they used a table to collate their findings. Below is an excerpt from their table collating the deconstruction of 12 of these advertisements:

What was free?	What was the cost?	Who was the intended audience/consumer?	What other products were supported/linked?
30-day subscription to Jenny Craig	Approx. $100/month for meetings/food	Females, middle-aged, white	Cellu-Sculpt; FreeCredit Report.com

As the students' work progressed, Diana and Lisa found, through conversation with them, that the students repeated that consumers should be aware of the advertising ploys of "free" promises. Observing the students' agile abilities to deconstruct these advertisements, and considering a discussion in the graduate content area literacy class about cycles of deconstruction and reconstruction, Diana then decided to amend the assignment so that each group of students also needed to provide a reconstruction of the texts. She provided them with two reconstructive options: the students could re-create the advertisement so that it more accurately represented its claims to its readers, or they could find alternative texts. Patrick, Rachael, and Denise chose to find online texts that provided diet and nutrition information to its readers without ensuing economic liability and attachments. Once they had amassed a collection of over 20 Web sites, they then decided to use only those sites that were maintained by nonprofit organizations. While they found that there were a few commercially produced sites that contained easily accessible, free, and well-researched information, they critiqued such sites for their inevitable links to products and services. As such, they decided to restrict their reconstruction list to those Web sites sponsored by nonprofit organizations and those that did not include hyperlinks to commercial products and services. In presenting their work to the class, Patrick, Rachael, and Denise showed the pop-up advertisements, the linked products and associated costs, and the nonprofit Web sites. In their conclusion, they had this to say:

Rachael: We decided to include free information about how to eat healthy and work out and stuff. So, here's a site [Denise shows a Web site using the classroom computer and data projector] from a university, and here's another [Denise clicks onto another site] from a chiropractor.

Diana: That's fantastic work, guys. Really well done. What made you decide to choose this bundle of pop-up ads?

Patrick: Well, they were absolutely everywhere, and then we started talking about how all of our moms had bought this stuff. So, we decided to ask them more about it and how they found out about it.

Diana: Oh yeah? What did they say? Was it from these kinds of advertisements?

Denise: Only my mom had bought something online, and that was the *South Beach Diet Cookbook*, but everyone else said they bought stuff from stores and found out about it through their friends.

Diana: So, do you think the companies behind the pop-up advertisements are wasting their money?

Denise: Nah, it's just that our moms don't really use the Internet that much, but I bet other moms do.

Lisa: You all keep mentioning "moms" a lot, and you said that women were the intended audience of these ads, but do you think it's more so moms than just any women? Or maybe a better question is what kind of person is being targeted by these ads?

[The three students look at each other and discuss this question for a little while before offering their answer.]

Denise: Yeah, we think it's more the women who have had kids and who are busy with other stuff that might buy stuff to help them be skinny like the pictures in the ads.

REFLECTION: PRACTICE INFORMING THEORY

After the day in which Patrick, Denise, and Rachael shared their work, Diana and Lisa debriefed the learning that had taken place. Overall, we both felt that the project sequence was quite successful, not only in engaging the students in critical literacy cycles of deconstruction and reconstruction (see Chapter 5 for discussion on this point) but also in supporting students' acquisition of skills and process relevant to digital literacy practices. In this lesson, the cycle of deconstruction and then reconstruction helped the students engage in critical literacy while also taking a strong stance about what texts would better reflect their particular worldviews and ideologies. As with the praxis example explored in Chapter 5, the students were more than capable of critiquing texts. In fact, it was their spontaneous critique of the pop-up advertisements that led to the more systemic inquiry into the texts and the production of alternative texts. While most of the groups chose to create advertisements that more accurately reflected associated costs with the promise of "free" perks, Patrick, Denise, and Rachael's collection of existing free Web sites was a refreshing application of reconstruction that did not require the authoring of new texts. These third graders demonstrated deftly that different texts capture differing agendas, representations, and appeals to their readers. By juxtaposing similarly themed but differently purposed texts, these three students demonstrated the dynamics possible in contrasting context, text, purpose, and interpretations in alternate texts.

By almost any measure of success, this critical literacy project had done well. However, reflecting upon the practice and its application of the theory is just part of what is required to achieve praxis. In asking what the theory of critical literacy could learn from this particular classroom application, one key issue arose.

CRITICAL LITERACY AND THE INSTITUTIONAL CONTEXT

This was the first time that Diana had asked her students to resist the reading of a text and attached this resistance to a more structured classroom activity with an outcome: the representation of the findings and the reconstruction to the rest of the class. Because of the newness of the questions and the structure of the assignment, many of the students were confused about what they were "supposed" to be doing. Initially, Diana found this frustrating and was afraid that perhaps being critical was not within the realm of these elementary students' cognitive development. We continued to talk about other pedagogical approaches that, while innovative, often are initially difficult because they ask that new conversational patterns and classrooms practices be engaged. In essence, when new practices and particularly new perspectives, such as critical literacy, are brought into the classroom, students are being asked to contend with a struggle between studenting (performing to the task) and learning (engaging in more authentic tasks). In essence, schools act as much as training grounds for particular kinds of behaviors as they do for learning. Students learn to perform in particular kinds of ways to garner positive attention and feedback from the teacher, adapting this to each new teacher. As the commonly held saying goes, one has to learn the teacher, not the subject matter.

As a case in point, Diana recounted how she had seen similar kinds of difficulties when she first placed the students in cooperative learning groups instead of working individually. The students had grown accustomed to working as individuals in their previous classrooms, and the expectations of small group learning were new to them. However, when the students learned that social acumen was an expectation of this teacher, they adapted. Although these students had only spent a few years in school, we found, as others have, that they had quickly learned to perform to the expectations of the teacher, and in fact, sometimes these learned performances overrode a different kind of learning that might be called for.

This tension between studenting and learning is particularly sharp in the praxis of critical literacy. Questioning and resisting standard and superficial interpretations of texts is at the heart of critical literacy. This, however, is a far cry from the historical implementation and interpretation of school-sanctioned literacy. For many students and teachers, this will present an odd if not uncomfortable fit between the context of schooling and the purpose of critical literacy. Put simply, schools are places of authority, and critical literacy often demands that the authority in the text be questioned. What does this practice of critical literacy have to offer for this tension between practice and theory?

In this classroom, the project in critical literacy came along well into the school year, after Diana and her students had the opportunity to establish the expected norms and values for that learning community. Because she valued community highly and also was sincerely interested in the lives and perspectives of her students, Diana's classroom enacted many of the ideals of democratic discourse. Within the context of the reading and writing workshop, there was a great deal of conversation and exchange of ideas about texts. This foundation carried over into the critical literacy exercise and, with modeling of what was expected, seemed to scaffold students' transitions to a new sort of perspective and interaction with texts.

In addition, Diana engaged in significant use of metalanguage, or language about language. As she debriefed with her students about the literacy exercise or practice they had just completed, they attached words and language to the skills, processes, and practices they were using. In fact, the focus of the critical literacy practice in this case was entirely upon just one word, *free*. As Diana and her students discussed what this word might mean and represent, they explored other useful vocabulary such as *intent, purpose, adjective, attachment, clause,* and *strings*.

This attention to particular uses of language and talk about language provided students with very real and tangible cognitive tools to use during the classroom discussions and presentations. As discussed in Chapter 4, the use of metalanguage is a requirement of critical literacy. In order to talk about how texts do their work and what they are trying to do to their readers, we need language to support this analysis. Whether it be the minute and highly analytic linguistic tools found in the research of scholars like Halliday and Hasan (1989) or in the more general debriefings that Diana conducted with her students, this "talk about talk" provides readers with the requisite distance and tools to examine texts. And germane to this issue of praxis, these tools become essential when tensions arise between the more normal and expected practices of the school context and those found within critical literacy. Theoretically, critical literacy asks readers to resist texts, and in practice, metalanguage provides readers with the scaffolding to engage with these expectations.

Using the model offered in this chapter where students conducted a critical deconstruction and reconstruction of the use of the word *free* in Internet pop-up ads, engage your students in a similar project aimed at critically analyzing discourse on the Internet or in other media (e.g., television ads, magazines, teenzines, ads in the environment, including billboards, T-shirts, hot drink sleeves). Use a grid or other system to plot the analysis and create a carefully thought out quantitative and qualitative critique. The following questions are guidelines:

- What word is featured prominently in the ad? (e.g., *free, healthy*)
- Who was the intended audience?
- What costs were involved in obtaining and using the featured product?
- What other products were supported or linked?
- What design features in addition to the product discourse were used to attract the viewer's eye to the product?
- Were there gender differences or elements present in the ad?

Finally, have students reconstruct this critique by recasting the ad in more helpful and truthful fashion or locating alternative ads that alleviate some of the pitfalls identified in students' critical deconstruction of their chosen ads.

DISCUSSION QUESTIONS

1. In Chapter 1, critical literacy is discussed as one of the four resources or processes that dynamic readers use to engage with texts. Along with code breaking, meaning making, and strategic use of texts, analyzing texts is a concurrent skill or resource, not one that comes after. Discuss how these skills can be best understood as concurrent rather than hierarchical.

2. In what other ways could critical literacy be used with younger readers? What kinds of texts could be used with emergent and beginning readers, and what types of questions would be helpful in engaging them in a view of texts as representational?

3. Is it appropriate to engage elementary-aged children in discussions of representation about race, class, and gender? Describe the specific politics of your local schools in taking these kinds of discussions.

RECOMMENDED FURTHER READING

Bloome, D., & Egan-Robertson, A. (1993). The social construction of intertextuality in classroom reading and writing lessons. *Reading Research Quarterly, 28,* 304–334.

Buckingham, D., & Sefton-Green, J. (1994). *Cultural studies goes to school: Reading and teaching popular media.* London: Taylor & Francis.

Comber, B., & Simpson, A. (Eds.). (2001). *Negotiating critical literacies in classrooms.* Mahwah, NJ: Lawrence Erlbaum.

Van Leeuwen, T. (2005). *Introducing social semiotics.* London: Routledge.

Vasquez, V. (2004). *Negotiating critical literacy with young children.* Mahwah, NJ: Lawrence Erlbaum.

REFERENCE

Halliday, M. A. K., & Hassan, R. (1989). *Language, context, text: Aspects of language in a social-semiotic perspective.* Oxford, UK: Oxford University Press.

CHAPTER 7

Praxis Point 3

Cycles of Deconstruction and Reconstruction

In the two previous chapters focusing on praxis, we explored several issues in the theory and practice of critical literacy, including being respectful of students' fandoms, employing critical literacy across the curriculum, and the tension in adopting a critical lens in traditionally hierarchical settings. In this chapter, we explore a last scenario of critical literacy praxis. This next scenario involves high school seniors and documents the highly valuable but complex implications of conducting critical literacy with issues that are both relevant and difficult in the lives of the participants.

SETTING THE CONTEXT AND PARTICIPANTS

At the time that this critical literacy project took place, Anna Foster was an English teacher in the small farming town of Albany, Nebraska. Anna was respected by both the high school staff and the town community as a knowledgeable and strict teacher. Although she had not grown up in a rural context herself, she had grown to love the familiarity and comfort of living, working, and socializing with a tight group of people.

In her role as an English teacher, she was responsible primarily for teaching mainstream and advanced courses to the high school's seniors. Anna's curriculum, as mandated by the district and correlated to the state language arts framework, was dominated by genre approaches to exploring both traditional and contemporary literature. In recent years, Anna had grown increasingly frustrated by being relegated to "cover" primarily fiction works with her students. While she was passionate about the interpretive and relational role that literature can provide to students, she also wanted to explore other kinds of texts with them while challenging them to read fine pieces of writing. One year, she decided to make such a shift. To do this, she made an effort to tap into one of her own interests that she heard echoed in her students' casual conversations, that of better understanding the substantive economic, social, and cultural changes that had swept this agricultural community in the past few decades.

As with many rural contexts worldwide, the population of Albany had witnessed significant changes in economy and lifestyle. Once marked by a healthy economy of family farms, the town of Albany now boasted many empty stores, a shrinking and aging population, and the presence of multinational corporations in the agriculture business. Anna's students had been told countless stories by their parents and grandparents about how things "used to be" and expressed emotions ranging from chagrin, regret, and disdain at the changes that had taken place, for many of them, before they were even aware of an alternative past.

Anna and Lisa observed the students' interests, their questions about the vanishing presence of small-family farming in the United States, and their knowledge of the large-scale agricultural factories and livestock operations dotting the countryside. Anna used this opportunity to engage the students with the book, and Lisa collaborated with them as they read the nonfiction bestseller *Fast Food Nation* (Schlosser, 2000). This exposé of the fast-food industry explores the implications of the industry upon many facets of both American and global economies, lifestyles, and culture. Included in Schlosser's explorations of the impact of the fast-food restaurant are topics such as the corporatization of agriculture and subsequent decline of the family farm, the mallification of America, the development of commercial marketing directly to children, and the health implications of this sect of food science.

Anna's students read the book and engaged in small group discussions with Anna and Lisa as they worked their way through it. As the students read the book and Schlosser's investigations into the ramifications of the fast-food industry on the agriculture economy, lifestyle, and ethos in the United States, they found many of the interviews and analyses not just relevant but insightful to their own lives. In particular, small group discussions held in Anna's class consistently centered on the decline of the family farm. While the students found that Schlosser had indeed represented a central feature of their lives, the lived reality of this economic and cultural pattern was something that was not fully developed in the book. The students decided to use their own lived experiences and ensuing knowledge to capture the local version of this large-scale story. In essence, the students were interested in taking up the same critical questions that Schlosser had applied to the industry of fast food, but they wanted to specifically ask these questions of the community of Albany and its history. They were interested in an inquiry project that would treat their community history as a text and engage with it critically, asking and exploring topics of benefit, advantage, marginalization, and costs.

To structure their inquiry, Lisa and Anna worked with the students to devise research strategies for exploring how and why the local economic base of family-based farming had shifted drastically over the past few generations. They used Schlosser's work as a model of inquiry, generating banks of questions that were used to interview elders in the community, community leaders, and others who had firsthand knowledge and experience with the transformation of the community. Somewhat similar to an I-search inquiry (Macrorie, 1988), the project was shaped to be a specific investigation into the agriculture industry's effects upon the small town of Albany. In this way, the project took up the basic process of an I-search project but with a particular focus upon using a critical lens to capture, describe, and interpret the findings.

As with the scenario described in Chapter 6, this project was also marked by a great deal of debriefing, stopping at each stage of the project to talk about the work the students were conducting and what they were learning along the way. This began with the initial stages of brainstorming who they wanted to interview and what questions they wanted to pose. As the students debriefed this stage, they found that they needed to do more explaining of the project than they had originally anticipated. This, in turn, helped them to refine not only why they were interested in this topic but also how it related to their schooling experience, particularly for English.

Students took 2 months to conduct and videotape the interviews. The 12 students in the class worked together to organize, edit, and narrate the findings from the interviews, combining their work into a single documentary about their inquiry into the local town that used to be Albany and how it had been changed, in part, by the shifting landscape of national and international agricultural trends. The process of videotaping and then editing the tapes brought up many questions of representation. In addition, the students, along with their teacher Anna, and Lisa, engaged in many discussions and debates about whether to include narratives by some of the students, in which they gave their own interpretations of the interviews and other relevant facts. In the end, the students decided to include these narratives, as they felt it was a more forthright representation of not only their perspectives in creating text but also how it impacted upon them as young people in the town.

Although clearly the work of amateur filmmakers, the documentary was poignant and relevant, and many students, in interviews, expressed that it seemed to them to be the first time they felt actively involved in the history of their community. One student, Deirdre, commented, "I've always just wanted to get the hell out of here, you know? I just saw it as a dead town. I still don't think that I could stay here and live and work here, but I've got a lot more respect for it and for my grandparents."

The final stage of the project was the sharing of the videotape. It seemed to be at best ironic and at worst a significant lost opportunity to just share the videotape with Anna, as the students' teacher. While this was technically a school-based assignment, simply submitting their video production for a grade in English class would have been to undercut the community-based relevancy that drove the project from its inception. In talking through options with the students, they voiced strong opinions that they wanted the video to be seen by others outside the high school.

The students were so proud of their work that they, along with Anna and the school administration, sponsored an evening showing. The students and Anna decided that one way of assessing a text is to have a wide variety of "readers" engage with it and gauge their responses. To that end, the students worked with the senior center in town, a staple and center of the town's aging population, to show the video one evening. The students developed a flyer to advertise the showing, emphasizing it as a record of local history and an investigation into the recent changes. They distributed the flyer at the senior citizens' center and churches and even posted several at the local baseball field. As the evening viewing approached, Anna noted that the students seemed to grow both more excited and nervous. She also felt a bit nervous—while she was a respected member of the community, she was actively opening up her pedagogical practices to this same community. While she had always advocated culturally responsive teaching, she had also grown accustomed to the freedom and license that teachers experience in their own classrooms.

The turnout at the evening viewing extended well beyond the local town, as young people, and adults from surrounding towns also, came to watch the short film. The students took control of the evening, with four to five of them taking turns to introduce the video and explain its creation and then helping to get conversations going after the video was shown. With coffee served after, the conversations in small groups consisted of lots of similar stories and emotions. For the most part, the audience members noted how much their own life stories were reflected in the people interviewed. They also commented upon the students' skills in creating the video. For a town that was still struggling to gain consistent Internet access, the production of this text by high school students was a point of pride and also instructive to their capabilities.

REFLECTION: PRACTICE INFORMING THEORY

As Anna and I worked through this unit, we were both humbled and impressed by the students' work. In their last semester as seniors, these teenagers exhibited commitment, research, and reflective thought that many would not see as probable in the warm months approaching their graduation. Without a doubt, the students engaged in an in-depth reading of a challenging work of nonfiction and then creation of their own narrative version of the local context. In fact, this project serves as a dynamic example of expanding our notions of what counts as text, helping students to be more critically aware of the choices they make as authors of texts and the implications of engaging in culturally responsive learning that is open to interpretation by the larger community.

This praxis example of critical literacy brings forth two key areas of further implication in using critical methods with texts: (1) Did this project "count" as critical literacy? and (2) How would we assess the students' work, with final grades looming around the corner and holding fairly high stakes in relation to high school graduation?

What Counts as Critical Literacy?

The practice of critical literacy is most tightly associated with choosing a single text and asking particular questions of it, including who is represented, who is not, who stands to benefit, and what is this text trying to do to me. In this situation, the students were not deconstructing specific multimodal or print-based texts. They were not cutting advertisements out of magazines and distilling the particular uses of image, layout, and text to reach a particular demographic. This unit did not explore the almost stock-in-trade questions of who is represented and who is left out with a single text, since we were not deconstructing particular texts per se. Instead, these questions were posed in a much larger sense.

However, this still felt like critical work to both the teachers and the students, so what was critical about it? The students had been deconstructing, all along, their understandings and readings of their community. Perhaps even more fundamentally, they were taking up the critical representation posed in *Fast Food Nation* and situating the relevance of that text within the local economy, culture, and history of Albany. Because most of them had grown up during a time when the economic boom of family farming was already a phenomenon of the past, they read Schlosser's exposé as an inquiry and deconstruction of their own lived but largely uninterrogated understandings of Albany. As they engaged in the research, interviewing, and production of their own documentary, the reconstruction and empowerment was palpable. While the effects of the documentary did not extend to disrupting the economic players in the agriculture business, it was not meant to. The documentary was the students' retelling of their reconstructed understanding of their community as a text.

In addition, this project brought up very real and lived critical literacy questions as the students constructed a representation of their own. While critical literacy questions of representation are most frequently posed during the deconstruction of text, they should similarly be taken up during the reconstruction and authoring of texts, or a key misunderstanding will take place that only the texts of others contain bias. For the students in this scenario, the prospect of including their own stated narratives was a key discussion that opened up issues of whose representation should be privileged in the video, explicit viewpoint of the author, and purpose of the video. In the end, the students decided that while all texts are biased, they wanted their own biases and perspectives to be "on the table," to use one student's words.

What counts as critical literacy is a question to be entertained from a reflective and open stance. Instantiations of critical literacy that are too similar or too narrow will necessarily delimit what this practice and theory can offer. Because critical literacy has as much to do with a way of viewing texts as specific questions, it must remain open and to a certain extent unnameable in a stoic sense.

ASSESSING CRITICAL LITERACY

In the current context of education in the United States, it is difficult to venture far into a conversation about educational practice without the words *accountability, assessment*, and perhaps even *value added* coming into play. And in particular, schools in contemporary policy contexts are saturated with the administration, scoring, and analysis of large-scale standardized assessments. How can critical literacy fit into such a context? In short, not very comfortably. Because democratic discourse and variances in plausible interpretations are hallmarks of critical literacy, this practice cannot be easily measured by multiple-choice questions. From the perspective of the authors of this book, however, this is an additional benefit that critical literacy can lend to education. Because critical literacy is both necessary to literacy pedagogy in an information age and incommensurate with measurement through standardized means, it reminds us that not everything desirable should be assessed through large-scale means. Rather, engaging in critical literacy means productively reengaging with questions of assessment of learning.

During the scenario described in this chapter, Anna and Lisa had many discussions about creating rubrics, scales, and portfolios of the students' work, but in the end, Anna decided that she would interview each student about her transformed understandings, her involvement in the documentary project, and then assign a grade accordingly. Not surprisingly, the students' grades were quite high, and also not surprisingly, the assessment took a distant second to the authentic assessment they received from their community at the documentary's evening showing. Just as exploring what a text is trying to do to its reader will engender a variety of responses, so should the practice and assessment of critical literacy.

REFLECTIONS ON CRITICAL LITERACY AS PRAXIS

Critical literacy in the classroom is neither a simple nor a well-agreed-upon venture. Not definable to any particular set of questions, activities, or texts, the snapshots from the past few chapters show the array of manifestations that can result from an overall view of texts as representational. The snapshots show a range of texts, including multimodal, community-based, and commercial, and they also show a range of approaches across different levels and grades of school. However, all three snapshots work from a basis of honoring students' literacy practices and allowing their interests to inform classroom practice. In this way, the snapshots, together, lend one last but crucial point of reflection: we are all already critical. Human beings engage in critical practice when two elements are present: (1) they are knowledgeable about the topic and (2) they are interested and even passionate about the topic. To assume that students need to be taught to be critical is to assume that there are not topics and content in which they are already imminently interested. As with all of us, we engage in critical practice when it serves our worldviews or when we are struck by such dissonance with our worldviews that we are moved to act. What these teachers provided to their students was the discursive space to engage in critical readings of text, the linguistic models of how to talk specifically about texts, and the reframing of texts to enact senses of agency.

While the snapshots described here are not provided as models of critical literacy, they do serve as actual practices that produced varying results. For some of the students, these practices were exciting, for others they were challenging, because they made such sharp departures from previous school-based textual practices. However, these three snapshots also demonstrate a crucial aspect that must be included in critical literacy practice: reflection. All of the teachers described here engaged in reflective practice, a professional approach to pedagogy that first motivated them to engage in critical literacy and the same perspective that kept their focus on praxis. They interrogated their practice with theory, and they developed their theories through their practice. This is precisely the type of practice that is essential to maintaining the productive space of critical literacy, one where easily defined and measured behavior and goals are not nearly as attractive as the complex, contested, and interpretive engagement with texts.

Up until now, we have been providing project examples, questions, and discussion points. However, at this stage of your efforts to have critical literacy be an integral part of your classroom, it seems appropriate to open the door to more creativity. Because the example in this chapter dealt with a crucial shift in the agricultural community of Albany, Nebraska, and the book *Fast Food Nation* (Schlosser, 2000), you may be inspired to try a similar project in your area. It probably won't take long to identify key issues in your town or community that could be considered more analytically and critically through the project initiated in this chapter. For example, the effects of globalization are far-reaching and poignantly described by *New York Times* columnist Thomas L. Friedman (2005) in the best seller *The World Is Flat: A Brief History of the Twenty-First Century*. In addition, various contemporary books, including *Don't Eat this Book: Fast Food and the Supersizing of America* (Spurlock, 2005) and a related film *Supersize Me* (Spurlock, 2005), also deal with the impact of our homogenized contemporary lifestyle on health. In essence, one doesn't have to search for long to identify issues worthy of students' attention and talents in critical literacy.

DISCUSSION QUESTIONS

1. One of the key aspects of the classroom snapshot featured in this chapter is the relevancy to community-based interests. In publishing their work, students felt a responsibility to create their texts so that they were accessible to community-based audiences. Revisit some of the ideas that you've implemented or are planning for critical literacy. What possible audiences could students reach with these activities? Be sure to discuss possible audiences outside the immediate school context. What effect might writing for other audiences have on the students' engagement with and production of texts?

2. Assessing critical literacy poses a unique challenge, particularly in the current context of federal mandates of high-stakes assessment. How can critical literacy be assessed? What kinds of approaches could you use to communicate students' abilities to analyze texts?

RECOMMENDED FURTHER READING

Comber, B., & Simpson, A. (Eds.). (2001). *Negotiating critical literacies in classrooms.* Mahwah, NJ: Lawrence Erlbaum.

Egan-Robertson, A., & Bloome, D. (Eds.). (1999). *Children as researchers of culture and language in their own communities.* Cresskill, NJ: Hampton Press.

Morgan, W. (1997). *Critical literacy in the classroom: The art of the possible.* London: Routledge.

REFERENCES

Friedman, T. L. (2005). *The world is flat: A brief history of the twenty-first century.* New York: Farrar, Straus & Giroux.

Macrorie, K. (1988). *The I-search paper: Revised edition of searching writing.* New York: Boynton.

Schlosser, E. (2000). *Fast food nation.* Boston: Houghton Mifflin.

Spurlock, M. (2005). *Supersize me.* (DVD). Hart Sharp Video.

Spurlock, M. (2005). *Don't eat this book: Fast food and the supersizing of America.* New York: Putnam.

CHAPTER 8

Critical Literacy and Educational Policy Texts

Through Chapters 1–7 we discussed theoretical bases of critical perspectives of text, redefining what counts as basic literacy, and some glimpses into critical literacy practices in classrooms. In education, however, there are three social fields that work with, alongside, and sometimes against each other: research and theory, practice, and policy. In these two final chapters, we explore the application of critical literacy to educational policy. Engaging students with critical literacy is one realm of practice, but policy can and should act as another text to be considered through critical lenses (see Chapter 3). In this chapter, we explore the potential of reading educational policy texts through critical lenses, using specific examples from the United States' federal policies on reading. The chapter considers policy analysis from a critical stance, along with contributions that complexity theory might offer this critique.

WHAT IS POLICY?

Why should we, as educators, who work at local levels, often far removed from the daily workings of official policymakers, be concerned with policy? While we often speak of research and practice and how to bridge the two, a third and equally significant component of our professional pursuits is policy, deliberately conveying to us, as educators, what to do, how to do it, and for what purposes (Edmondson, 2004). Policy is defined as the captured essence of values

(Ball, 1990). In this way, policy serves no less an important function than communicating what kind of literate subject of the state is to be nurtured through schooling (Luke, 2002). At all times, the government should be and is concerned with what type of literate citizens is needed for society and how schools can best work to produce these characteristics in their students. As educators, we should similarly be interested in what is conveyed to us through policy. However, this is not to suggest that educators should have a simplistic reading of educational policies that direct them. In keeping with the tone of critical literacy, we should regard all policies as representational and subject to critical readings, so in this chapter we explore what representations might be best served by literacy policy.

Policy serves to communicate values (Stone, 1997). The crystallization of values in policy is brought to fruition in both explicit and implicit ways. Explicit statements about what counts as literacy, goals in creating literate subjects of the state, and related guidelines about assessment and reporting all comprise readily accessible literacy policies. However, policies can also be conveyed, sometimes quite explicitly, through speeches and images, as values and shared understandings of those values are complex aspects of policy, mediated by words, images, and actions (Lingard, Henry, Rizvi, & Taylor, 1997). To explore what literacy policies might include, then, we must address questions of what is explicitly communicated through statements, guiding reports, as well as what is conveyed through more informal communication. All of these sources communicate messages about what is possible, what is not possible, by whom, and on whose behalf.

CRITICAL POLICY ANALYSIS

Policy analysis, examining the purpose, fruition, and other aspects of policy, runs the gamut from simple cost-benefit analyses to complex questions of inducements, rules, facts, rights, and powers (Edmondson, 2004; Stone, 1997). These analyses are necessary, as policies can simultaneously limit our options as teachers and open up possibilities for pedagogy and curriculum. To that end, we present next a specific policy analysis of current federal policies regarding reading, using a federally sponsored meeting, and then, in the next chapter, we present one school's initial conversations about this policy. Throughout both discussions, the policy and its surrounding conversations are working to decide what is possible for children, teachers, and their work in literacy.

First presented and examined is the initial presentation of the federal government's then-new policy regarding early literacy. Throughout the course of this 3-day series of meetings, various speakers from research universities, schools, and the federal Department of Education spoke about the purpose, content, and parameters of a new funding initiative and policy relevant to reading instruction in the United States.

Critical Discourse Analysis and Educational Policy

Conversations and texts from this context were explored using **critical discourse analysis** (Fairclough, 1989, 1992). Critical discourse analysis is a qualitative research method best used to analyze the purpose, function, and impact of textual practices in various contexts. It shares many theoretical bases with critical literacy and is therefore an appropriate tool to use for critical policy analysis. In particular, this stance toward policy, one that asks who the policy benefits and how, is one that is useful for educators interacting with district, state, and federal policies that impact their daily professional lives. Because policy works to crystallize values, it is appropriate for invested stakeholders, including administrators, teachers, students, and parents, to question if the represented values are congruent with their own.

Using critical discourse analysis to examine policies provides opportunities to interrogate these represented values through the language used to name and describe the policy. This methodology emphasizes the social and political groundedness of the language and texts (Gee, 1996). It sees all texts as situated in social, political, economic, and cultural spaces. For example, a policy that addresses educational opportunities and limitations for immigrants reflects the political forces and influences of the context. To examine these situated texts, critical discourse analysis focuses its attention on both large, or macro, features of language such as the kind of text being used as well as more finite, or micro, features of language such as tone, semantic choice, and other grammatical tactics. In so doing, this methodology pays attention to micro aspects and functions of linguistic markers while trying to connect these linguistic choices to the larger social, political historical fields where these texts interact with each other.

Using discourse analysis affords opportunities to examine the relationship between the language and patterns used in various settings relating to language and literacy and the possible ways of being constructed therein. Specific to this application of critical discourse analysis, the perspective provided the crucial opening to question which aspects of being a student, a teacher, and a literate person were authenticated, silenced, marginalized, and subverted within these policy spaces.

NATIONAL DISCOURSES

On February 20–22, 2002, over 100 state-level educational administrators gathered in Washington, DC, to learn about a new funding initiative launched by the U.S. Department of Education to improve reading achievement in the early years of schooling. In defining what counted as policy documents and discourse during the 3 specific days of the federally sponsored gathering, named the Reading Leadership Academy, lines were blurred between the authority found in the exact wording of the Reading First grant application and bylaws and that found in the speakers' presentations and handouts. The meetings consisted of a brief introduction by then Assistant Secretary for Elementary and Secondary Education Susan B. Neuman and then a series of speakers addressing (a) Reading First Initiative (2002) and grant opportunity, (b) Early Reading First Initiative and grant opportunity, (c) accountability, (d) effective instruction, (e) reading programs, (f) professional development, and (g) assessment. At the time of this meeting, the final draft of the grant applications had not yet been released, but meeting participants were urged to use all of the information presented to inform their applications, prompting another participant at the meeting to comment, "It doesn't matter if it's in the law or just in their presentations; it's what we're supposed to say in the application." To that end, Lisa used both the wording of the draft of the grant and the discourse and handouts from speakers to conduct a discourse analysis (Gee, 1999), with the aim of identifying the cultural models proposed for the reader, the teacher, the reading program, and the institutional or policymaking entities. Examining the discourse of the speakers was particularly important, as it was via those speeches that participants came to understandings of what was important for the funding opportunity and for the policy. These same participants, then, would be the initial conveyers of this information, through their own representations, in their home states, districts, and schools.

As a state reading specialist, Lisa attended this 3-day Reading Leadership Academy, one of three sponsored by the U.S. Department of Education in early 2002. What Lisa heard, read, and saw during these sessions formed a partial basis for this discourse and critical policy analysis of the Reading First Initiative, part of the reauthorized Elementary and Secondary Education Act.

During the first hour of the meeting, the audience watched a video that combined translucent images of the American flag rippling in the wind superimposed over pictures of young children reading aloud. The powerful images intertwined patriotism with classroom use of language to support the instruction of reading. These images were punctuated by rousing music and the words of the male narrator, who told the viewers that "freedom is threatened when so many are not learning to read." Such high-stakes discourse and ideology demand consideration, from an educational research perspective, of several questions: (a) How was the federal government defining reading? (b) What was left out of that definition, and what information would be supplied to this group of state bureaucrats, administrators, and specialists? and (c) How would this information enable, constrain, and support their work at shaping literacy policy and practice in their respective states, districts, and classrooms?

The basic premises and key messages of the academy are key to understanding the potentialities of the policy. Because all of the speakers who presented during the course of the 3 days drew participants' attention to using "what works" and based that unitarily on "scientifically based reading research," the policy was premised on what we might term *functionalist* assumptions, which presuppose that schools—all of their other possible, debatable, and contestable educational purposes, practices, and consequences aside—in the first instance and final accounting are sites for the most "efficient" production of measurable, behavioral skills. This type of premise, however, ignores the ideological, historical, social, and political nature of any policy (Marcuse, 1964). Moving beyond overly simplistic and falsely apolitical questions of what works, a critical policy analysis poses essential questions of what works for whom, by whom, and for what purposes, bringing to conscious levels issues of hegemony, privilege, and marginalization (Edmondson, 2004). In this way, the policy and the speeches around it drew upon the close dialectic between language and power, as theorized by Foucault (1979). He drew our attention to the divergent ways in which power relations are linked to the constructed part of the collective substance of society and how subjectivity is constituted through these power relations. One of Foucault's major premises was that contemporary governments control power through their control of knowledge, which is communicated through language. In this case, how the policy named and located the functionalist purposes of literacy, in fact, how it defined literacy, works to create and to close possibilities for people who appropriate and work under the policy. In concert with critical theory and critical literacy, this perspective of language and knowledge posits that all linguistic renderings of knowledge are implicated with power differentials. However, Foucault cautioned against nihilistic and fatalistic views of power, instead invoking power relations as also comprising the intention to teach, to shape activity, and to provide imprints of self-awareness and identities. Simply put, truth is constructed through and to benefit various relations of power, but power can fluctuate across persons, moments, and spaces. By simply reading against a text, such as educational policy, power can be invoked by multiple participants. In this way, Foucault's theories provide a useful theoretical grounding for examining the propagation of pseudo knowledges or ideologies through the Reading First policy and surrounding discourses. In fact, one argument of critical literacy, and one that applies to this critical policy analysis, is that engaging in critical questions of a text, assuming an oppositional reading stance, is one way of enacting agency.

Because this policy analysis focuses strongly on the texts, both oral and written, that were shared during the 3 days of the meeting, speeches and printed artifacts comprised the sources of the data. In the discursive analysis, Lisa used samples to discuss what was present and what was missing from each of these areas. Analyzing what is missing is often just as important as the more conventional practice of analyzing what is there. Often, when a specific text does not address a topic, it removes it as a viable option, interpretation, or nuance (Luke, 1997), thus building through inclusion and omission crucial axes of truth.

For the discourse analysis, samples were chosen largely on the basis of their representation of converging and compatible points, their coverage of both oral and print discourses from the meetings, and their typicality of linguistic details found in the speeches and handouts. Close examination of the discourse of public speeches and artifacts provided in those three days was used to ascertain how this particular policy defined the cultural models of the reader, the reading program, the teacher, and the governing agency. The following is a compacted version of a more detailed analysis previously published (Stevens, 2003). In reading through this analysis, keep in mind that just like the policy that it is deconstructing, this interpretation is just that: an interpretation. While it is critically informed by knowledge and background both in literacy pedagogical foundations and policy studies, it is nonetheless an interpretation. In reviewing this critical policy analysis, consider the critical stances that you take up with this policy and how that might differ from what is found in this one.

The Reader

One might assume that a clear definition of reading would be pivotal to any substantive discussion on language and literacy and the policy and funding of reading instruction. Antithetically, an explicit statement of the definition of reading was never provided during the course of the 3-day meeting. However, this is not to say that meaningful messages about reading were not communicated. On the contrary, consistent subtextual messages were conveyed. Consider four specific but convergent references to reading made during this Reading Leadership Academy:

"We want every child, and I mean every child, reading by the end of third grade" (Neuman, 2002).

"Every student should read, read well, and on time" (Hunter, 2002).

"In later grades, once children have foundation reading skills [*sic*], the focus of assessment shifts to fluency and reading comprehension" (Kame'enui, 2002).

"The number of words [read] per minute is a pretty good indicator of comprehension down the road" (Kame'enui, 2002).

These utterances build a cultural model of the young reader being promoted in the Reading First policy. By cultural model, we mean a figuratively painted image of what it means to be a competent reader, what defines competency, and how it is ascertained. This model, one that was situated uniquely within the context of the Reading First Initiative but traversed time-space hybridizations to local, school, and community-based realizations through the enactment of the policy, was being applied to every single child in the United States. The cultural model of the reader is one who must, by the end of third grade, be able to orally decode at least 120 words per minute (Hunter, 2002; Kame'enui, 2002). This quantification was repeated more than a dozen times in speeches and printed words throughout the meetings. This goal is constructed as universally applicable to all students, regardless of particular contexts. In fact, the only critical descriptor that defines children's expected reading ability is their chronological age. This implies that the ability to read happens, or can be made to happen, simultaneously for all children, as a function of their purportedly identical biophysical development. From this cultural model of a reader, what counts as reading is an end-sum artifice, namely the ability to decode enough words per minute.

Antithetically, over the past three decades, comprehension has been purported by many researchers working from diverse paradigms—cognitive, psycholinguistic, sociolinguistic, ethnographic—to be the ultimate purpose of any literacy activity (see Chapter 1). Research from across these wide disciplines, in investigating how children become proficient readers, has situated meaning making as a core element to the longitudinal process of becoming a proficient and critical reader. However, in this Reading Leadership Academy, comprehension was reserved for "later grades" and seen to be an automatic consequence of proficient oral decoding fluency by the end of third grade.

What is left out of this cultural model is the image of a complex reader, one who mediates his or her differentiated engagement with different types of literacy events, for different purposes, and with different results. While many different models and descriptions of proficient readers exist, Freebody and Luke's (1990) Four Resources model offers a compelling comparison because it consciously includes the historical, political, and social nature of reading texts and because it has been institutionally sanctioned in the policies of the state Department of Education in Queensland, Australia (State of Queensland, 2001).

Freebody and Luke (1990) proposed that a proficient reader in New Times (Luke & Elkins, 2000) must be able to simultaneously engage four distinct but dynamic practices: (1) code breaker (coding competence), (2) meaning maker (semantic competence), (3) text user (pragmatic competence), and (3) text critic (critical competence).

The picture of a reader created in the Reading First policy consistently addresses the code-breaking practices and marginally references the meaning-maker practices, but only then as an automatic consequence of decoding ability. Completely lacking from the Reading First policy is any allusion to the pragmatic and critical resources that proficient readers must draw on to expertly use and create texts. This absence is particularly acute when considered in light of the unprecedented convergence and confluence of digital and print texts in today's multimediated contexts (Lankshear & Knobel, 2002). In other words, an oral reading fluency aptitude as framed in the discourses of Reading First will not suffice in determining the purposes, interests, and nuances in books, Web sites, streaming video, e-mail messages, and myriad other multimedia text outlets. The multiliteracies enacted with these print and digital texts (New London Group, 1999) are not reconcilable with the Reading First policy.

The absence of processes beyond code breaking is also salient when considered in light of the growing numbers of culturally and linguistically diverse students in classrooms in the United States. Through the sole and overly emphasized attention on the code-breaking aspects of reading, the Reading First policy also reifies a normative view of reading, one that prioritizes consistent performance of code-breaker behaviors. Through this emphasis on repetitive behaviors and the assumed superiority of Standard English, the policy promotes a singular linguistic version of reading competence. In other words, under this policy, readers can only be considered proficient if they are able to decode fluently words in Standard academic English. This kind of definition works in two ways to colonize students: it reproduces a monocultural and monolingual version of competency, and it silences spaces for fluency in other registers. Situated within the increasingly diversity of language and culture in today's schools, this colonizing pedagogy is one that tries to smooth over the variations in backgrounds found in a diverse student population, to produce similar subjects of the state (Gutierrez, 2002).

The analysis of how the reader is defined in this policy is considered through both what is contained in the definition and what is left out. While veering toward a myopic focus on what could be commonly named as a bottom-up approach, the policy forgoes the critical features of being a reader in order to prioritize a stripped-down version of competency. However, while this critique is valid from the perspective of the field of literacy, there are also critiques to be considered by situating the policy in political, economic, and social contexts.

The implications of a sparse definition of reading are impactful when considered with the demographic shifts in U.S. populations, thus maintaining more fundamental skills without the loss of meaningful acquisition and learning of and through language (Eskey, 1988).

The Reading Program

While an explicit definition of reading was not provided, reading programs enjoyed an obvious and exalted status throughout the speeches addressing the Reading First policy. One speaker (Hunter, 2002) advised the participants that their first and most critical role as leaders was to "fully implement a comprehensive research-based reading program." This single statement was repeated almost 10 times in the handouts provided to participants and voiced no fewer than a dozen times during this speaker's presentation alone. In fact, she asked the participants to read aloud the sentence with her at the start of her presentation.

In the portion of the meeting that was specifically titled "Reading Programs," the focus of the context was primarily showing examples from "good programs and bad programs" (Eichelberger, 2002; Robinson, 2002). While copies were not provided to participants due to copyright issues, examples from good programs displayed on the projection screen were those that used synthetic phonics approaches and included direct quotations, or a script, for teachers. As explained by Eichelberger, examples of bad programs were those that referenced cueing systems in addition to and beyond graphophonics and those that did not provide teachers with explicit words to say to the students. Not only is the actual language of such presentations condescending to an audience of professional educators, specifically senior state administrators (e.g., "good" versus "bad"), but it provides evidence of reductionism in assessment of variable strengths and weaknesses of approaches to literacy. The implication of this argument is that *any* program that is teacher directive and with a strong coding focus has virtue and that all others are somehow deficient in theory, evidence, and practice.

Throughout the hundreds of times that the word *program* was mentioned in speeches and the handouts provided to participants, it was invariably accompanied by either *comprehensive* or *scientifically based* and usually both. What is present throughout these references is the commercially published, prepackaged reading program as the inanimate authority in reading instruction. Only those programs that espoused a synthetic, phonics-based approach were anointed as "good." While the specific wording of the draft copy of Reading First calls for proposals without referencing specific approaches and strategies, the presentations that comprised the bulk of the meetings focused on reading programs.

By name, Open Court and Direct Instruction were lauded through anecdotal stories provided by several of the speakers (Ephraim, 2002; Johnson, 2002; Mahmoud, 2002; Whelchel, 2002). Clearly, the reading program was the only qualified entity for reading instruction. Because of its pervasive presence, it appeared to be the panacea that would act as the great equalizer in creating fluent decoders by the end of third grade.

Through the exaltation of the reading program as monolithic panacea and the invocation of the administrator as faithful enforcer of the use of the program, Reading First began to situate administrators and policymakers in clear roles again—not stated explicitly but converging through the various comments and utterances in the meeting. These roles are ones of surveillance, monitoring, and control. Foucault's theories about the regimes of power in contemporary times suggests that the Reading First policy firmly defines the state agency as the central panopticon (Foucault, 2000), the all-seeing, omnipresent central surveillance of classroom behavior and activities.

If the state is positioned as agentive panopticon, it relegates the cultural model of the teacher to the subject of the state, one to be surveilled and controlled. In fact, during these meetings about literacy pedagogy and curriculum, particular and explicit attention to teachers was noticeably muted. The meeting presentation titles included topics on leadership, reading programs, and assessment but nothing specifically about the role of the teacher, requisite knowledge of the teacher, or epistemologies of the teacher necessary to promote literacy achievement. This makes sense when the reading program has already occupied the place of prominence, expertise, and authority in the discussions of reading instruction. Again, consider the following quotations from academy speaker Moats (2002), who addressed the participants on the topic of professional development:

> Professional development courses and coaching aim to support the adopted, comprehensive reading program; implement state standards and frameworks; present the consensus findings of reading research. . . .
> Teachers don't want endless choices. They want structure. They want fewer choices. They don't want to invent their own curriculum. They want to know what works. . . .
> The teachers told us that when you don't have someone coming into your room to observe, you don't give your best effort.

Through her words, Moats paints the picture of a teacher whose job is to closely follow the reading program, reading the script. The teacher here is portrayed through narrative and anecdote—quite a departure from the "scientific evidence" orientation of the policy. This is a teacher who "wants" products, who won't deliver unless surveilled by the panopticon, who declines engaging in the rich, substantive, and sometimes confusing complexities of literacy development, and who is externally motivated to maintain the appearance of instruction.

While Moats also emphasized the need to provide teachers with time to talk and time to establish professional development at school sites, these aspects were to provide forums for further talk about how to faithfully implement the reading program. In that sense, professional development is to occur, again, under the gaze of the panopticon of the surveilling power and serve the regime of truth presented by the reading program. In fact, it could be argued that in relation to the reading program, the teacher is situated as an extension of that commercially produced and sold product. In this way, the teacher is firmly situated as an object of the state, and the state and commercial entities are conflated as having dominant power/knowledge controls over the teacher, the student, and their interactions in the classroom.

The Reading First Initiative, as communicated through the meetings of the Reading Leadership Academy, offered only narrow definitions of reading, prescriptive approaches to reading programs, and constrictive roles for teachers. Definitions of reading are limited to code-breaking skills necessary to be a fluent oral decoder, leaving out processes and practices of comprehension, pragmatic use of text, and critique of text (Freebody & Luke, 1990). Curricular choices are restricted to commercially published phonics programs and are then cast in the overly simplistic binary of either good or bad. Teachers are lauded as professional only if they remain faithful to the letter of the scripted reading programs.

While any federal funding opportunity is that, an opportunity, there were distinct lost opportunities to draw upon compelling and converging areas of literacy research that should inform current practices, policies, and beliefs. The privilege afforded to code-breaking skills, a necessary but insufficient component of literacy, is inconsistent with the recent surge in literacy research that acknowledges the complex array of skills, processes, and practices necessary for today's text-saturated world (New London Group, 1996). A discursive analysis of the spoken texts introducing Reading First yields this limited view of literacy, along with narrow cultural models proposed for the panoptic role of state agencies and administrators, technicist and reductionist roles for the teacher, and subjugated roles for the students. However, what remained to be seen from these meetings and the swirling discourses about reading programs and scientifically based reading research was how the policy would be taken up, co-opted, resisted, and interpreted in institutional and local contexts.

MOVING FROM NATIONAL TO
LOCAL: COMPLEX CONNECTIONS

To examine the ways in which the Reading First policy was mediated by teachers and students in one local context, we drew upon critical policy analysis and certain aspects of complexity theory to account for both the inherent plays of power and control and to resist teleologic assumptions and analyses of policy trajectories.

Traditional approaches to policy analysis have emphasized pragmatic and reductionist questions of efficacy, with assumptions made that efficacy is understood through the purported goals of the specific policy (Lingard et al., 1997). Critical policy analyses foreground questions of cost and benefit, but with a particular eye to the social relations of power, knowledge, and hegemony (Ball, 1990; Edmondson, 2004). In this way, a critical policy analysis assumes that with any given policy, some will stand to benefit while others may be hurt, marginalized, subjugated, and/or silenced. Complexity theory reminds us that how change occurs in complex settings is never predictable, unidirectional, or unitarily felt (Davis, Sumara, & Luce-Kapler, 2000).

Traditional examinations of policy have also worked from theories, scientific principles, and epistemologies that assumed linearity in systems. This linear thinking model, based on the notion of predictability, stability, and control, was an honest attempt by analysts to know and understand how the systems react to policies and how to maximize positive instantiations of those reactions. By contrast, complexity theory addresses the behavior of complex, nonlinear, most quintessentially unpredictable systems.

Complex systems are characterized by nonlinear and often unpredictable relationships between cause and effect; small changes can have large effects, large changes can have minor effects, and not all things in the system are weighted equally. In fact, a complex system is, by definition, made up of differing components that work together to unique results. Learning settings bear striking resemblances to complex systems. Classroom teachers are, by and large, practiced and efficient at resisting large-scale reforms and agendas, while the highly structured systems of schooling can provide insurmountable obstacles to even minor innovations. Now consider how, invariably, teachers and administrators are faced with several concurrent agendas and policies. One can see immediately the dramatic increase in the complexity of the context and its various factors. In Chapter 9, we maintain a use of critical policy analysis but apply it to one specific school's interaction with this policy, to see how various readers interacted with this text.

Critical Literacy and Education Policy

Although teachers are not often encouraged to engage with policy texts from critical stances, many teachers already do this. Just as with young people who are not innocent dupes of popular culture, many educators read and interpret new policies based on their past experiences and with critical perspectives. The following are just a few suggestions on structuring crucial literacy perspectives with educational policy.

- Compare the scope and sequence of two commercial publishers' reading programs. What kind of a reader is likely to be encouraged by each? How do the practices encourage readers to be code breakers, meaning makers, pragmatic users of texts, and text critics? What role is the teacher afforded in theses programs?

- Consider how you can become involved with educational policy in your school, district, or state. Are there openings to participate on textbook adoption boards, educational policy committees, or library committees, for example?

- Consider how you can become involved with educational policy in your professional organizations (e.g., International Reading Association, National Council of Teachers of English). Are there openings to participate in special interest groups or educational policy committees, for example?

- Does your educational institution explicitly support social justice? Where is this seen and enacted? How could this perspective be built into the mission?

RECOMMENDED FURTHER READING

Edmondson, J. (2004). *Understanding and applying critical policy analysis: Reading educators advocating for change.* Newark, DE: International Reading Association.
Stevens, L. P. (2003). Reading First: A critical policy analysis. *The Reading Teacher, 56,* 662–672.

KEY TERMS FROM THIS CHAPTER

Critical policy analysis is an orientation toward policy that uses questions of what works for whom, by whom, and for what purposes, bringing to conscious levels issues of hegemony, privilege, and marginalization. Similar to critical literacy, it is particularly focused on ways that policies enact possibilities and constraints for differing segments of the population.

Critical discourse analysis is a qualitative research method best used to analyze the purpose, function, and impact of textual practices in various contexts.

REFERENCES

Ball, S. (1990). *Politics and policymaking in education.* New York: Routledge.

Davis, B., Sumara, D., & Luce-Kapler, R. (2000). *Engaging minds: Learning and teaching in a complex world.* Mahwah, NJ: Lawrence Erlbaum.

Edmondson, J. (2004). *Understanding and applying critical policy study: Reading educators advocating for change.* Newark, DE: International Reading Association.

Eichelberger, J. (2002, February 21). *Reading programs.* Speech presented at the Secretary's Reading Leadership Academy, Washington, DC.

Ephraim, R. (2002, February 21). Untitled. Speech presented at the Secretary's Reading Leadership Academy, Washington, DC.

Eskey, D. (1988). Holding in the bottom: An alternative approach to the language problems of second language readers. In P. Carrell, J. Devine, & D. Eskey (Eds.), *Interactive approaches to second language reading.* Cambridge, UK: Cambridge University Press.

Fairclough, N. (1989). *Language and power.* New York: Longman.

Fairclough, N. (1992). *Critical discourse analysis.* London: Longman.

Foucault, M. (1979). *Discipline and punish: The birth of the prison.* Harmondsworth, UK: Penguin.

Foucault, M. (2000). *Power* (J. D. Faubion, Ed., R. Hurley, Trans.). New York: The New Press.

Freebody, P., & Luke, A. (1990). Literacies programs: Debates and demands in cultural context. *Prospect: Australian Journal of TESOL, 5*(7), 7–16.

Gee, J. P. (1996). *Social linguistics and literacies* (2nd ed.). New York: Routledge.

Gee, J. P. (1999). *An introduction to discourse analysis, theory, and method.* London: Routledge.

Gutierrez, K. (2002). Studying cultural practices in urban learning communities. *Human development, 45*(4), 312–321.

Hunter, P. C. (2002, February 22). *Accountability.* Speech presented at the Secretary's Reading Leadership Academy, Washington, DC.

Johnson, S. (2002, February 21). Untitled speech presented at the Secretary's Reading Leadership Academy, Washington, DC.

Kame'enui, E. J. (2002, February 20). *Effective instruction.* Speech and paper presented at the Secretary's Reading Leadership Academy, Washington, DC.

Lankshear, C., & Knobel, M. (2002). Do we have your attention? Attention economies and multiliteracies. In D. E. Alvermann (Ed.), *Adolescents and literacies in a digital world*. New York: Peter Lang.

Lingard, B., Henry, M., Rizvi, F., & Taylor, S. (1997). *Educational policy and the politics of change*. London: Routledge.

Luke, A. (1997). The material effects of the word: Apologies, stolen children and public speech. *Discourse, 23*(3), 151–180.

Luke, A. (2002). What happens to literacies old and new when they're turned into policy. In D. E. Alvermann (Ed.), *Adolescents and literacies in a digital world*. New York: Peter Lang.

Luke, A., & Elkins, J. (2000). Editorial: Special themed issue: Remediating adolescent literacies. *Journal of Adolescent & Adult Literacy, 43*, 396–398.

Mahmoud, E. (2002, February 21). Untitled. Speech presented at the Secretary's Reading Leadership Academy, Washington, DC.

Marcuse, H. (1964). *One-dimensional man*. Boston: Beacon.

Moats, L. (2002, February 22). *Professional development*. Speech presented at the Secretary's Reading Leadership Academy, Washington, DC.

Neuman, S. B. (2002, February 20). Untitled. Speech presented at the Secretary's Reading Leadership Academy, Washington, DC.

New London Group. (1996). A pedagogy of multiliteracies: Designing social futures. *Harvard Educational Review, 66*(1), 60–92.

Reading First Initiative. (2002). Retrieved from www.ed.gov/policy/elsec/leg/esea02/pg4.html#sec1201

Robinson, J. (2002, February 21). *Reading programs*. Speech presented at the Secretary's Reading Leadership Academy, Washington, DC.

State of Queensland. (2001). *Literate futures: Report of literacy review for Queensland schools*. Brisbane, Australia: Author.

Stevens, L. P. (2003). Reading First: A critical policy analysis. *The Reading Teacher, 56*, 662–672.

Stone, D. (1997). *Policy paradox: The art of political decision making*. New York: W. W. Norton.

Whelchel, B. (2002, September 21). Untitled. Speech presented at the Secretary's Reading Leadership Academy, Washington, DC.

CHAPTER 9

Critical Policy Analysis in Local Contexts

In the previous chapter we used critical policy analysis, a perspective that employs the theoretical and practical aspects of critical literacy and focuses them on policy texts. Included in these texts are both explicit, print-based versions of the policy and the more informal conversations that interpret the policy. This analysis was located at the federal level, when the policy and its intentions were first represented to stakeholders from the 50 states. However, in keeping with a more dynamic definition of policy (a crystallization of values), the manifestations of this policy did not end at this meeting. Rather, the policy can be understood to have continued in widely dispersed districts, schools, and classrooms. In this chapter we turn our attention to one school's interaction with this policy. In maintaining a focus on critical policy analysis and its applicability to education, we ask more context-specific questions of how the policy was represented, understood, taken up, and resisted.

Policy texts are often practically understood to be artifacts contained in legislative documents, court proceedings, and bylaws. However, policies can be more broadly defined as the crystallization of values and representations of differing stakeholders' views of what is important to a government and what is negligible. From these definitions, it is easy to see how policy enactment begins rather than ends with the completion of a formal document or announcement. Rather, how, in this case, educators interpret and interact with policies also falls within the parameters of policy and should be considered from a policy analysis approach. However, crucial to this more broadly drawn approach is a consideration of the ways in which policies and texts can connect over time and space. In this case, the policies that were discussed at the Reading First meetings in Washington, DC (see Chapter 8), will be taken up, modified, rejected, and recast in different, hybrid versions of what was originally presented at the federal meeting. By hybrid we mean that these conversations at the local level will include some aspects of the original texts, but there will be additions, deletions, and references to other texts. In this sense, the federal policy discourse and discussions will undergo time-space hybridizations of local, institutional, and societal discourses (Leander, 2001). These time-space hybridizations indicate that while the handouts and speeches of the federally sponsored meeting were delivered at a specific time and context, the words, the ideas, and the manifestation of the policies would impact schools, classrooms, teachers, and students, traveling well beyond the meeting, crossing time and space boundaries, and shifting across these contexts. Along with a discursive analysis of the cultural model of a reader propagated within the discourse of the policy, this analysis also draws upon classroom observation and interview data to explore the complex ways in which the policy was enacted in local contexts. Although one key concept is understanding the hybridity of policy interpretations, another key concept is seeing these related policy discussions as intertextual, combining aspects of these texts along with other texts, or policies. No policy comes to teachers without being preceded by lots of others, so the ways in which we make sense of, and potentially critique, educational policies is in mind of other policies that have come and gone. In considering and critiquing policies, then, we do so in mind of other policies, or texts, creating an intertextual understanding of the policy at hand.

By drawing upon two dialectic exchanges about the same policy, we note how different instantiations of a policy can be manifested through discussion, echoing, fracturing, and altering meanings. Although these conversations took place in wholly different times and spaces, the dialectic meanings made connect to each other in myriad ways. In a Bakhtinian (1981) sense, the participants at the federal meeting and the local school-based staff were engaged in an asynchronous, heteroglossic construction over what teachers should do to support young children's language and literacy development. The particular language used in both settings, then, is paramount in providing a purview about these potential meanings. Understood from sociocultural perspectives of semiotics, these representations are offered as a source of intertextuality, all exploring the various meanings made of reading, literacy, teaching, and accountability. Bakhtin defines intertextuality as

[t]he property texts have of being full of snatches of other texts, which may be explicitly demarcated or merged in, and which the text may assimilate, contradict, ironically echo, and so forth. In terms of production, an intertextual perspective stresses the historicity of texts: how they always constitute additions to existing "chains of speech communication." (p. 94)

This understanding of intertextuality helps to explain how the texts at the federal level can be seen as linked to but not synonymous with the enactments of these policies at the local level. And while our analytic focus has shifted from Washington, DC, to a more regional location, a key undertaking of this critical policy analysis is further understanding how power and governmentality work through formal and informal policy documents.

POLICY AND GOVERNMENTALITY

Policies, broadly construed and narrowly enacted, act as a key technique of the state, communicating what is meant to be done by educators on behalf of the government. In this way, administrators, teachers, and students draw upon explicit policies to see what type of literate subject the state is creating. Social theorist Michel Foucault (1979) discussed developments in the 20th century that have created states of governmentality. Governmentality works as individuals read and understand what is expected of them by the state or hegemonic entity and then gradually begin to surveill themselves in meeting those expectations. A noneducation example here might help to explain how governmentality and internalization can work. In this case, consider a weight loss company and its approach to having customers and clients come to group meetings, weigh in to obtain their current status on the diet plan, share successes and stories, and then monitor their own food intake until the next meeting. While no one from the company would be monitoring clients' food consumption, customers would self-surveill, with the understanding that they will have to share their experiences at the next meeting. While this is a fairly innocuous example of internalization of controls and rules, governmentality can be understood to work the same way. An example might be if a school district mandated that teachers should coordinate and reference their lesson plans according to the governing collection of learning outcomes. Although the district officials might not be dropping in to "check" for this practice, teachers might engage in a kind of self-checking or self-surveillance in anticipation of a check from the district officials. Understanding governmentality is important in contemporary society, because even though the policy might not be explicitly monitored, the implied presence of the state and its surveillance can exert influence beyond immediate presences. Therefore, in analyzing policies from critical stances, we are only concerned with not just the types of ways the policy is enacted, but how it comes to be understood through conceptions of the government. We now turn our attention to one school's exploration of the Reading First policy. As you read through the events and conversations that unfolded at this meeting, keep in mind how past educational policies have been introduced to you at your school and the reactions to these policies.

LOCAL CONVERSATIONS

Goldberg Elementary School is an inner-city public school in a large city in the western United States. The school's population of students is extremely diverse, with children coming from over 25 different ethnic backgrounds. Nineteen languages are spoken by the school's children, along with a common nonstandard dialect of English. By and large, the children in this school do not have home languages and cultures that map closely onto the typically white and middle-class culture of schooling (Delpit, 1995). The teachers in this school are mostly female, white, and come from middle-class backgrounds.

The school has recently been named as a struggling school, having had its students score below the desired levels of percentage on a standardized test. The school now must choose a reform model to overhaul its practices, particularly in the area of reading and literacy. At the time of these interviews with staff members and documentation of staff meetings, the school's faculty was engaged in various reactions to the impending mandate of the reform model. Some teachers spoke of leaving the school, others placed hope in the reform model to help them succeed with the school's students, while still others talked openly of ways to resist the reforms and in particular the reading agendas of the federal government.

About a month after the Reading Leadership Academy was held in Washington, DC, Christa Goodson, who was a second-grade teacher at Goldberg Elementary School, and her fellow teachers attended a staff meeting in which her principal related information about the new funding initiative as it had been explained to him at a monthly administrators' meeting the previous week. In the school meeting, the principal introduced the policy to the teachers and spoke of it as possibly providing more funds for the school and being able to use those funds along with the reform program. The following is a brief excerpt from transcripts (Field notes, April 17, 2002) of that meeting:

Terry [the principal]:	I know you guys will not like this, but the funding seems to be attached to one of the reading programs.
Christa:	Which ones?
Terry:	Well, they didn't tell us specifically, but probably, you know, the normal ones like DI [Direct Instruction] and SFA [Success for All].
	[Audible protests and groans from the teachers in the room]
Terry:	I know, I know, but this is what we are facing. We are going to have to choose a reform model, and I'm also just telling you about the other monies we might get for a reading program.
Joyce [second-grade teacher]:	So, we are just supposed to get rid of all the leveled books, the guided reading, the workshop stuff? That all just goes out the window?
Terry:	I'm not saying that, and I'm not sure. Maybe we could find a way to get a program and fit it in with the practices we already, um, do.
Christa:	Or, maybe we could get the money, buy more books with it, and keep doing what we know works best for the kids.
Danielle [a first-year teacher of first grade]:	I hate to be the one to disagree, but I actually like the idea of getting a reading program. I need some kind of structure, and I feel like I'm not getting it done with my kids. Maybe the program would be better.
Christa:	That's not the solution to that problem.
Terry:	OK, OK, look, we're not, um, going to solve this right now. I just want to let you know so that you are not surprised if it happens down the road.

In this staff meeting, many of the nuances and tones from the Reading Leadership Academy have been carried through to a local context. The funding is accurately linked to particular commercially published reading programs, and the principal talks about the school as responsive and subject to the external forces of this funding opportunity and other policy pressures. However, what is apparent in just this first discussion around the Reading First policy is the resistance from the majority of the school's teachers. The discussion quickly moves to a resistant exploration of ways to work within the parameters of the policy but for different purposes and with different activities. In this way, the teachers and this principal are searching for ways to escape the panoptical gaze of the state agency.

In an interview following this staff meeting (Interview, April 23, 2002), Lisa asked three teachers on the faculty to participate in follow-up interviews and classroom observations. Included here are conversations with Christa, one of these teachers.

Christa has been teaching early primary grades for over 20 years and describes her philosophy of literacy pedagogy as "balanced," resulting from many years of reflective practice, observation of her students as they develop their literacies, and "a few worthwhile inservices." She uses a mixture of a center-based approach to literacy activities and the Four Blocks method (Cunningham & Hall, 1996). She is regarded as a leader in her school and is often consulted by the principal about pedagogical and curricular decisions for the school. She was asked to participate in this study because of her well-articulated beliefs about literacy pedagogy and her forthright commitment to children's critical literacy development.

Christa:	Well, in some senses, it's the same thing all over again. They think that they know how they want us to teach, but it does seem to be getting more and more restrictive all the time.
Lisa:	You said "they." Who's the "they"?
Christa:	Well, this time it's the feds, but normally it's the state department.
Lisa:	OK, so sorry. You were saying they know how you should teach reading?
Christa:	Yes, but we've all seen these swings of the pendulum before. Now it's back on phonics, but it will swing back after they figure out that our ESL kids can imitate the reading program but understand nothing of what they've read.
Lisa:	So then you think the policies will shift back toward more holistic approaches?
Christa:	Well, that's what they do—swing back and forth while we have to keep the balance going in our classrooms and get no help with the real problems.
Lisa:	Like what? Which problems are those?
Christa:	Well, like just the languages. My Spanish has gotten a bit better, and we're starting to get more Spanish resources in the classrooms

and library, but I've got a student who just arrived from the Philippines, and I've got nothing for her to read. You tell me how asking her to go "fa fa fa" [imitating the repetitive oral decoding graphemes found in many reading programs] is going to help her.

Lisa: OK, so what will you do if you are asked to use a scripted reading program?

Christa: I honestly don't know. I cannot imagine getting rid of my centers and standing in front of my kids and reading to them what someone else has told me to say. I just don't know. It depends on how strict it is, but my friends who teach in other schools just scare me with how it works in those schools. It's like completely scripted and broken down into each minute. I honestly don't know why they need a teacher to do it. They could get anybody because you just follow the directions. Sort of like a recipe.

Lisa: Do you think there's room for you to resist the program?

Christa: There might be. Like with this bunch—they are so good, you know? We can do the scripted stuff, and I can talk to them about how the centers are better, and they'll get that, but what if I can't do centers at all with the group next year? Then I can't compare it to anything. That's all they'll know.

Lisa: Mm hmm. So if you can, you'd like to get your kids to critique the program?

Christa: Yeah, like we do with most things. But I don't know how to do that if the program takes up all of the minutes in the day, and I'm not sure who's going to enforce it.

Lisa: What do you mean?

Christa: Well, you know, you shut your door, and then you do what you like. Terry's really good about that. He doesn't want to know all the dirty details, but he knows that lots of us will just continue to do our own thing when no one's watching.

Lisa: But you're concerned about your ability to do that within a scripted reading program?

Christa: Yeah, because they make the whole school do it, and everyone switches kids for the reading time, so it gets harder to do your own thing.

Through this conversation, Christa explores the difficult position that has been constructed for her through the Reading First agenda. She is frustrated but not surprised at the lack of recognition of teachers' expertise and knowledge in the policy. Neither a simple obedient subject of the state nor a rebellious ideologue, Christa seeks ways to tease out workable regions within a restrictive literacy policy. In this way, Christa enacts a critically literate stance with the policy. She situates the policy within her immediate context, engages with it critically, and then reconstructs the implications of the policy in negotiation with her own epistemologies and values.

In particular, Christa names the panoptic gaze of the policymakers and the state agencies as a force to be restricted. She understands implicitly that the policy falls within a central and centralizing role of government as surveillance, and she searches for ways to resist this particular aspect of the program. In this way, she is probing for tactics that she can use to resist the larger strategies of the policies. De Certeau (1986) discusses tactics as the ways that people resist the controlling strategies of larger entities and discourses. In this conversation, Christa is actively engaged in hypothesizing the efficacy of a few different tactics, and works within the limits that serve to draw boundaries around possible material realities of the policy.

Yet, within the same school, Danielle is likely to seize the opportunity that a scripted language and literacy program offers to her as a frustrated beginning teacher, one who does not have confidence in the same levels of teacher-based knowledge and proficiency as does Christa. Terry may acquiesce to the policy pressures of a reform program and a scripted reading program, but he is searching for borders to work within the governing forces while creating spaces for his teachers to grow in their professionalism. Together, this school acts as an irregular fractal within the implementation of this literacy policy. Nuanced and varied, the reaction to this policy problematizes concepts of learners, literacy, and pedagogy. This problematization extends far deeper than the platitudes conveyed around the Reading First policy. In that way, the policy contradicts the complexity in this local context. Instead of offering salient direction, the policy places strict behavioral demands on educators while attempting to quash substantive thought and dialogue around the relevant issues of literacy pedagogy, curriculum, and assessment. How, when, and where, we might ask, is the failure of government educational policy documented and reported, through which discourses and texts?

Interrogating literacy policies is something that needs to be done, in concert with critical theory, with a strong regard for particular contexts. Simply shifting the focus from reductionist definitions of literacy to critical literacy would not suffice. If the federal, local, or state government swiftly changed its position and moved to make critical literacy its policy du jour, this would actually depart little from the successive fads, agendas, and reforms that school-based practitioners learn to expect from their governing agencies.

In fact, critical theory and critical literacy have purposefully worked from the margins. If we were to simply recommend that the policies be shifted to include critical literacy, we would be working in opposition to the nature of critical literacy, which is to see all texts as representational. In that sense, what is not so crucial is the precise nature of the policy as a stand-alone text; rather, what might be more fruitful is to explore what processes and practices are enacted with policies as texts. Along these lines, while a policy might include critical literacy, this representation would be insufficient in holding up the ideals of critical stances without also seeking to encourage critical literacy as a practice. So, while a shift to critical literacy definitions would certainly help to shift focus and perhaps even open up further discussions, two other major shifts would need to take place in the roles afforded to teachers interacting with policies and the role of the policy itself.

TRANSFORMING POLICY INTERACTIONS

As can be seen through Christa's and Joyce's responses to the news of the Reading First federal funding policy, teachers are not often afforded opportunities to actively engage, interpret, and transform educational policies. In typical hierarchical fashion, policies are devised, encoded, and transmitted from persons removed from local teacher/student contexts. These district, state, and national policies crafted by well-intentioned and competent professionals, represent only the top layer of the complex agents involved in daily educational practice. If the only people who can inform and transform policies are those who work outside of classrooms, this has the double effect of devaluing educators who work with students and making policymakers' roles imminently challenging because of a decontextualization.

Policies might remain initially devised and enacted by those who work in offices that affect several specific contexts, but they must be regarded as incomplete without cycles of discussion, interrogation, and transformation by the people who will ultimately work with these policies: the administrators, teachers, and students whose lives are most affected by the policies. This kind of permeability would require, first and foremost, time for discussion. As Britzman (2003) has noted, teachers who are relegated to work within the rugged individualist discourse, and this comprises most educators (see Chapter 3)—are delimited from professional growth, their own and others'. Policies need the professional input of teachers, and dualistically beneficial, teachers need to be more than the recipients of values crystallized by others. These conversations are best taken up, from a critical stance, in the particular contexts where they will be enacted. In fact, it makes sense for teachers to engage in critical policy analysis as a first step to enacting and understanding critical literacy. Asking students to engage in critical literacy without first doing so oneself is, at best, a risky venture. Without having worked through the complications that arise from choosing texts to deconstruct and how to reconstruct them, teachers may not have an experiential understanding of the promises, pitfalls, and gray areas of doing critical literacy. However, while this chapter holds implications for teachers to conduct critical policy analysis, there are also reconstructive recommendations that can be made from this deconstruction. There are responsibilities that policymakers should consider in crafting educational policies. In the following section, we discuss more productive frameworks that can be used in designing educational policies.

EDUCATIONAL POLICY AND COMPLEXITY THEORY

The school context, like other settings, is a complex one. It acts unpredictably, is made up of disparate features, and defies unidirectional flows of knowledge and directives. In fact, as any teacher knows, planning a unitary lesson for a class of students will inevitably lead to advantaging some students while marginalizing others. Just who will respond and how, though, is often quite unpredictable. Enacting and working with policy is no different, in that it is seeking to devise what precisely should happen, in what order, and by whom for settings that are inherently unpredictable.

How can policymakers learn to cater to the complexity of learning settings? Drawing upon the work of Davis, Sumara, and Luce-Kapler (2000), the elegantly simple concept of enabling constraints offers a compelling alternative to the overly didactic and regulatory tone of Reading First and many other policies. Instead of policy that seeks to rein in the synergistic possibilities of human beings in complex settings, an alternative might delineate a few constraints, restrictions, or goals and then allow for divergent, creative, and necessarily unpredictable pathways to those goals. Such a fundamental but significant shift would transform interpretation of a policy from an exercise in obedience and/or resistance to one that seeks relevant, impactful, and inventive fruitions. As government policies forge their strongest alliances with large corporations, the need for accountability cutting both ways has never been higher. However, with demands for accountability must also come reconstructive efforts to envision language and literacy policies differently.

DISCUSSION QUESTIONS

1. What educational policies have you seen enacted and then abandoned? With your other group members, discuss the reasons for the short shelf lives of some educational policies. In what ways are the local and national contexts of education political fields?

2. Have you ever resisted an educational policy or seen others do so? In what ways did this resistance take place? What was the outcome of the resistance?

3. What are the potentials for engaging in critical policy analysis at your school? Consider factors like the tenor of the current administration, the shared values of the teachers, the most pressing issues of the school, and the surrounding community.

REFERENCES

Bakhtin, M. (1981). *The dialogic imagination: Four essays* (C. Emerson & M. Holquist, Trans.). Austin: University of Texas.

Britzman, D. (2003). *Practice makes practice: A critical study of learning to teach* (2nd ed.). Albany: State University of New York Press.

Cunningham, P., & Hall, D. (1996). *The four blocks: A framework for reading and writing*. Clemmons, NC: Windward.

Davis, B., Sumara, D., & Luce-Kapler, R. (2000). *Engaging minds: Learning and teaching in a complex world*. Mahwah, NJ: Lawrence Erlbaum.

De Certeau, M. (1986). *Heterologies: Discourses on the other*. Minneapolis: University of Minnesota Press.

Delpit, L. (1995). *Other people's children*. New York: New York Press.

Foucault, M. (1979). *Discipline and punish: The birth of the prison*. Harmondsworth, UK: Penguin.

Leander, K. M. (2001). This is our freedom bus going right now: Producing and hybridizing space-time contexts in pedagogical discourse. *Journal of Literacy Research, 33,* 637–680.

Glossary

Agency: refers to students feeling like they have a voice in a classroom and their opinions and views are valued.

Attention economy: the use of print and digital texts to capture consumers' attention in order to sell products.

Content area literacy: teachers' efforts to guide students' understanding and critique of all forms of texts (print and digital) in subject areas such as English, science, social studies, mathematics, art, music, and physical education.

Critical discourse analysis: a qualitative research method best used to analyze the purpose, function, and impact of textual practices in various contexts.

Critical literacy: active questioning of the stance found within, behind, and among texts. Critical literacy is an emancipatory endeavor, supporting students to ask regular questions about representation, benefit, marginalization, and interests.

Critical media literacy: a predisposition to examine how print and nonprint texts (e.g., film) serve to construct our knowledge of the world and related social, economic, and political positions people occupy. Given the increased visual element in contemporary forms of digitized text, critical media literacy can include a careful grounding in visual media literacy and semiotic design as a basis for critique. Semiotic design involves paying close attention to the sign systems commonly used in print and nonprint texts, including fonts, diagrams, symbols, and other elements (Van Leeuwen, 2005).

Critical policy analysis: an orientation toward policy that uses questions of what works for whom, by whom, and for what purposes, bringing to conscious levels issues of hegemony, privilege, and marginalization. Similar to critical literacy, it is particularly focused on ways that policies enact possibilities and constraints for differing segments of the population.

Critical reading: an orientation toward reading that arose out of the liberal-humanist philosophical tradition. Critical reading places an emphasis on skill-based tasks such as distinguishing fact from opinion and, at the more advanced level, recognizing propaganda in texts. The critical reading stance supports the idea that meaning resides in texts to be deduced through careful exegesis.

Critical theory: a broad epistemic framework that can be found in many fields in the social sciences and humanities. Generally, these arenas share in common a critique of dominance, a commitment to emancipation, and the use of critique and reflection as means to empowerment.

Deconstruction: the analytical process of examining any form of text as non-neutral in terms of race, class, and gender issues, biases, hidden agendas, philosophical underpinnings, and other elements of power in discourse.

Democratic classroom: a democratic environment in which participants engage in deep discussions about difficult questions related to power, agency, rights, and harm (Harper & Bean, 2006; Parker, 2003).

Digitally mediated texts: texts in hyperspace, on the Internet, on iPods, and on other nonlinear presentation modes that are typically more fluid than traditional static print.

Emancipatory education: a dialogic approach to education, in which teachers and students work together toward goals and objectives that counter political, economic, social, and cultural marginalization.

Essentialist label: a narrow, often stereotypical view of a person reduced to a single term like *skater* that purports to identify and describe identity.

Fandom: a subculture consisting of individuals who share a common interest, such as an author, a hobby, or a genre.

Identity formation: identity is more than some unified concept, because people have multiple identities in varying social contexts, thus challenging older, narrow definitions of identity.

Intertextual: meanings that are constructed when reading and interpreting a text but mediated by meanings from other texts, including books, CDs, conversations, movies, and video games.

Metacognitive awareness: literally, thinking about thinking and being aware of how digital texts function in the information age.

Metalanguage: critical conversations with students about language in terms of what work texts accomplish through word choice, structure, and underlying elements that go beyond the content of the material.

Policy analysis: examining the purpose, fruition, and other aspects of policy.

Positionalities: looking closely at how a text "positions" a reader in terms of race, class, gender, perspective taking, and insider versus outsider perspectives.

Praxis: the blend of theory and practice that mutually interrogate each other.

Reconstruction: the process during which readers recast the text from a different perspective, find alternative texts that privilege different voices, or create their own text. Any of these options are taken up with explicit and democratic discussions of what kinds of representations are more preferred, suitable, and appropriate with the particular sets of values, practices, and purposes. Through reconstruction, readers return to texts with the conscious decision about the type of representations that resonate with their worldviews and experiences.

Reflexivity: a constant, cyclical questioning of the theoretical basis, practical implementation, and overall impact of literacy practices.

Scientifically based literacy: a classical, modernist faith in measurable objectives and test data in conjunction with literacy instructional practices related to behavioral psychology, including scripted lessons, enabling activities, and direct teaching.

Semiotic: a signifying system that includes words, images, and sounds upon which producers and consumers of text rely for meaning making.

Socially situated literacy practice: all literacy events, including reading and discussing various forms of texts, are ultimately layered with power dimensions in a classroom, so that some students have a presence in discussions while others are silenced due to varying social status, race, class, and gender perceptions and biases. Like a text, no social situation is neutral.

Stance: the orientation one takes when interpreting a text.

Subject positions: a discursively organized way of being in the world and seeing oneself against the backdrop of possible social positions and practices advanced in various forms of texts. This is a complex notion of identity that recognizes multiple identities and views of the self against a normalized, homogenized, externally produced standard (e.g., the ideal achieving student as defined by grade point average success).

Texts: now broadly defined as cultural tools that include a host of print and digitized forms serving a multitude of purposes (e.g., instant messaging, text messaging, using a smartphone, viewing streaming video, listening to books).

Text genres: identifiable patterns of texts, including narration and expository text patterns (e.g., compare/contrast, problem-solution, chronological listing, pro-con).

REFERENCES

Harper, H. J., & Bean, T. W. (2006). Fallen angels: Finding adolescents and adolescent literacy in a renewed project of democratic citizenship. In D. E. Alvermann, K. A. Hinchman, D. W. Moore, S. F. Phelps, & D. R. Waff (Eds.), *Reconceptualizing the literacies in adolescents' lives* (2nd ed., pp. 147–160). Mahwah, NJ: Lawrence Erlbaum.

Parker, W. C. (2003). *Teaching democracy: Unity and diversity in public life.* New York: Teachers College Press.

Van Leeuwen, T. (2005). *Introducing social semiotics.* London: Routledge.

Index

About the Authors

Lisa Patel Stevens is Assistant Professor in the Lynch School of Education at Boston College. Before taking up this position, she worked as a researcher and lecturer at the University of Queensland, a state literacy specialist in Hawaii, a literacy consultant, and a reading teacher in public schools in Nevada and California. Throughout her career, she has explored literacy as a sociocultural practice in particular contexts, particularly among young people in their secondary years of schooling. In addition to this coauthored book, she has coedited a book exploring the cultural construction of adolescence, *Reconstructing the Adolescent: Sign, Symbol, and Body*. In addition, she has several published articles and chapters in various kinds of publications.

Thomas W. Bean is Professor in Literacy/Reading and Coordinator of Doctoral Studies in the Department of Curriculum and Instruction, College of Education, at the University of Nevada, Las Vegas. He is considered a leading scholar in content area literacy. He is the coauthor of over 18 books, 25 book chapters, and 95 journal articles. He was recently honored with the College of Education Distinguished Faculty Research Award for his studies of students' discussions of multicultural young adult literature in content area classrooms. He is coauthor of recent books, including *Content Area Literacy: An Integrated Approach* (9th ed., 2007) and *Targeted Reading: Improving Achievement in Middle and Secondary Grades* (2004), devoted to addressing strategies for meeting No Child Left Behind requirements and test preparation. He is also a coauthor of the International Reading Association position paper *Adolescent Literacy: A Position Statement*, designed to guide policy decisions aimed at increasing literacy development efforts for adolescents.